The Black Woman

by
Dr. Robert E. Willis

THE BLACK WOMAN

by Dr. Robert E. Willis

In *The Black Woman*, author Dr. Robert E. Willis tackles a difficult subject: the physiological, economic, social, and psychological makeup of the black female. He embraces similar aspects of the white male and female, if not indeed, of the entire human family. The purpose of this book is to point out some of the strengths and weaknesses of "this marvelous creature," and by so doing, make the whole black race stronger and more competitive in the white world.

Dr. Willis essentially deals with differences between the black and white races—morally, physiologically, socially, economically, and psychologically—by uncovering the roots of the problem. He often refers to the "missionary way" in sexual relations. From there, he traces its effect to the present day, to the detriment of the black race, on the physiological makeup of both the black man and woman, as well as the white man and woman.

In *The Black Woman*, Dr. Willis presents a fascinating thesis that should excite the intellectually inquisitive of all races. The book is enlivened by keen insights and thorough research.

Contents

Perhaps no woman in the world or no living being over the years has been pictured with the feeling of strength that has been alluded to by playwrights, authors, etc., as generously as has the "black woman."

It is the purpose of this book to bring out some of the reasons for this strength and to point out some weaknesses of this marvelous creature and, perhaps by adjusting to this knowledge, hopefully make herself an even stronger individual, and consequently make the whole black race stronger and more competitive in this "white world."

For it has been the black woman in America, perhaps more than any other single individual or group of individuals, who has triggered the major social and economic changes for the better, undisputedly so between blacks and whites in this country.

And only through her indestructibility have we as a race, and perhaps this country as a nation, been able to survive.

For in her bosom, her womb, her introitus, her wisdom, she has nurtured and strengthened black and white men, women and children.

Hopefully, this book will give a peek into what makes her "tick."

Introduction

This book was written to try to explain the problems of black America, particularly the relationship between black America and white America. I hope that in no instances will this book ever be interpreted as a "put down" of any group or any particular race, but rather that it will be beneficial as a reflection, to bring on a better life for everyone concerned. Under no circumstances will this book go into the relative mental differences between the races. Basically, I feel there are none, and if there are, so many other compensatory things will equalize them that it is a moot point.

It is my fundamental belief that one of the major factors that has been hampering blacks in America is that they are subjected to morals and laws that are foreign to their basic culture and genealogy. What I am saying is that this is literally a white's world. The whites have developed certain morals and laws in Scandinavian and northern countries that befit white individuals in an environment of snow and ice and occasional sunshine. Whites have keen noses and white skin; their basic genealogy, or basic heredity, is totally different than that of the blacks. The whites brought these morals and cultures over to the New World and set them down as laws, laws that the blacks had to follow. Blacks, however, are not physically equipped to follow these white laws and morals any more than the whites are equipped to follow the laws of a tropical-originated culture of black-skinned people.

Blacks have had to modify their whole way of life, their health, and their social ideology according to white rules. This was very difficult. Doctors who are trained in this country are trained to take care of white people, even black doctors. Blacks, therefore, who do not approach physically and mentally the attitude and physical build of the majority, the whites, find themselves in a particularly compromising situation. It is easier for light-complexioned people, on a physical and mental basis, to make it. With this in mind, if we reflect on our surroundings, we can understand how it is most difficult for most African-like individuals to find their way or to reach a position of power in this country. As one becomes blacker, as one becomes more African-like, and as one deviates from the "white norm" of blond, blue-eyed, etc., one has to live under certain handicaps, handicaps which are additive the more one deviates from his norm. This fact may account for the tremendous extra money spent by blacks for hair straightening and skin lighteners and hair dyes.

Perhaps of more controversy than anything else are the I.Q. tests in this country which may determine the destiny of many individuals. Here, too, the black man is short-changed in western society; there is no way possible that he can compete with whites in I.Q. tests made up by whites. There are certain basic genealogical mind patterns of thought that the individual or culture has which the individuals who make up the tests have in common with the individuals who take the test.

Contra-wise tests that would be made up by test designers of African origin would result in better test scores by individuals of African descent over those of white descent. I strongly believe that there are certain genealogical hereditary patterns in each individual's brain which are potentiated through centuries of similar inbreedings by races. Therefore, an I.Q. test is a very poor index if we are judging pure intelligence.

I, as a black individual who has never heard Swahili, would probably be in a better position to understand it than a white individual of similar inherently equal I.Q. Likewise, a white individual who had never heard one of the languages from the north would be better able to understand it than I because of this basic genealogical hereditary brain pattern. In the lower animals, these patterns are automatically passed on through the species. This is best illustrated by salmon going upstream to spawn.

As this book progresses, I will postulate the basic reasons for this. I think all through the book it is evident that one of the problems is that the black leaves home with certain handicaps—physical handicaps and, perhaps, mental handicaps, engendered by the fact that he or she is living literally in a white world.

Another thought in this book that should be considered is that over the years Marcus Garvey and other black leaders have wanted blacks to go back to Africa or have a separate state. This book will offer some insight into these "back to Africa" movements of the great black men. I think that all of these men felt that something was wrong with the black and white relationship in this country, and that the solution was to go to Africa. I do not think these black men recognized that the big factors were the cultural and physical differences between the two races and other problems that have worked to the disadvantage of the black race in a white-cultured society.

THE BLACK WOMAN

THE BLACK MAN'S EARLY SURVIVAL

In the beginning, we have to consider these physical
differences. We should start with Darwin's basic theory of
selection of species to help understand such differences on
a scientific basis. My interpretation of Darwin's theory is
that over the years, species survived due to heredity and
environment by virtue of the fact that the male or female has
attributes that tend to enhance the positive aspects of the
race in its environment and that the male and female who best
adapt to their environment mate, and thereby produce offspring who are more adaptable to the environment. Thus,
environmental conditions affect heredity or the individual's
basic genealogy. One of the classic examples is the beautiful plumes of the male peacock. The more attractive he is to
the female peacock, the more she will desire him, and the more
he will breed. This basic rule goes all through the animal
kingdom. Not only does it embrace beauty, but it also embraces physical and mental attributes, as well as the social
attributes, and their relationship to their environment. The
more powerful a man is physically and mentally, the more he
has a tendency to be the leader; therefore, he will breed
more and will have superior children and will help to procreate a stronger race. This can be seen, basically for this
book's purpose, in the female development.

As a further point of controversy, we can reflect on the
attitudes of the black man and the white man toward life. I
think that along the same line of reasoning, the white man,
born in the cold climate and subjected to winters of six or
seven months in his basic genealogy or heredity, had to prepare for it. In February or March, when food ran out, he would
have starved to death if he had not prepared.

On the other hand, the black man, who literally bathed
in milk and honey in tropical surroundings, knew that, regardless of what happened the next day, the sun would shine, the
bread loaf would be there, the fowl in the air, the fish

1

would be in the sea, and the animals on the land would be plentiful. So it was not necessary for him to kill or hoard great amounts of dead animals, for they would only rot. It became a part of the black man's genealogy or heredity that he did not become a killer or hoarder as was necessary with the white man. It became part of the white man's heredity to hoard because those who did not, did not survive in their harsh environment. So this, too, is a factor, if we can accept Darwin's theory of selection of species: how the climate plays a role in the development of differences over thousands of years.

During the course of living, one philosophizes; but basically, we are here to be born, procreate, and then die. We are here to procreate our species primarily. Like all other animals, it seems that this is the only justification for our being here on earth. But more to the point, many black marriages, in this situation that we find ourselves, become bogged down in the social laws and morals of the white man. The black man is basically a polygamous individual; the white man is a monogamous individual. I will explain why there are physical reasons for both situations. I think that in the natural habitat of the black man, he finds that nature has developed a system whereby there are more black females to black males at the age of procreation than there are white females to white males in the natural habitat of the white man. At least more black females reach maturity proportionally. I feel that this fits into the total picture of survival.

As the sun dominated the black man's environment, it encouraged the survival of the blacker individuals, of individuals whose hair was kinky, both characteristics to best equip the survivor, the procreator, with the tools to protect himself from the sun's direct rays. The wide nose perhaps enabled him to breathe in more hot air and cool it to the 98.6-degree internal environment that is the same for all humans.

On the other hand, the white man in a relatively non-sun, cold environment was developing a hairy body, whiter skin, more subcutaneous fat, straight hair that could fall down over his neck and face to protect him from the cold elements, and, of course, the keener nose to reduce the amount of cold air and also to warm it to fit the bronchial tree at the 98.6-degree internal environment.

We can go on and on comparing the outward physical differences between the two races; to compare the mental attitudes between the two races is probably the toughest job-- but here goes.

If we can conceive of a situation in which the white man has to prepare himself for the long winter, we can understand that through successive generations he probably developed a mental genealogy of being a great individual for planning, etc.; on the other hand, the black man, having to use his mentality to survive in the split-second dangerous jungle, probably developed a quicker mentality than his counterpart. This "jungle man," this quick-witted ability to survive any situation, probably led to the black man's downfall in slavery in this country, for it was not the slaver, totally, who kept the black man in chains; it was the black man's own inability to plan ahead. For in his genealogy, his quick wit always kept him dominant over his previous surroundings from day to day. Being brought to a cold country where planning is absolutely essential for survival placed the black man in an impossible situation. His own mental capabilities kept him bound in slavery. For instance, he would escape, but, alas, he would have to return to the plantation, for he did not hide a barrel of beans in the woods or have extra clothes and blankets stashed away for the strange weather that he now encountered.

As we rush into a socialistic situation, the planners will no more be in demand than the quick-witted individual who has to make snap decisions in the fast-paced society that we are entering. Sports are a good example of how the mental and physical genealogy of the black man are becoming more dominantly evident, that is, sports in which winter weather is not preeminent.

The wide nose allows more air to enter the lungs in a stated time, allowing the heart to pump less, etc., whereas keen noses allow a limited amount of air through the nostrils, therefore increasing the heart's activity. To compensate for this, keen-nosed individuals in the heat of competition often open their mouths for air and further defeat themselves by breathing through a nonspecialized area, therefore making more work for the heart, etc. Although I am not certain, I do think that through genealogy, the black-skin sweat glands, oil glands, etc., are better able to throw off heat in "the heat of competition," thus sparing the heart's work load. This ability to sweat not only led to his enslavement in the cotton and sugar cane fields,but also led to his recent employment in the foundries, tunnel construction and "sweat shops" in the north. As progress continues, we will see "quite wittily" highly reflexive thinking is extremely necessary in such areas as basketball, football, surgery, etc. Indeed, as pollution continues, the black man's physical plant will be able to survive even more as whites flee to the suburbs, the mountains, even the moon, just to breathe. For the moment, however, the black will continue to buy his Cadillacs on a $7,500-per-year income, for he is a "jungle man," a survivor from day to day.

3

THE YOUNG BLACK FEMALE

Due to our more recent past, during slavery and following slavery, when the black female was always projected in a light above the black male, certain consequent things affected us. During slavery, quite often the black female was the mistress of the slaveowner, a maid in the "man's" house. She became a little higher in her station than the black male. This black female became a dominant figure in the male-female relationship because she received favors from the master, and she could literally have the black male subjected to a considerable amount of punishment. Of course, as slavery ended, the black female often acted as a buttress between the previous white master and the black male.

Consider a young black male child in a fight with a white child during slavery and afterward. For some reason, the black child may have gotten the best of the fight; he would run home to his mother and father. The mother would have to give anything available, including her body, to the white man to keep him from whipping her son. We can see a situation in which the black female went out to meet the white man and, either through promises or whatever, would console him, while the black male would be hiding under the bed or would take to the woods until the white man's temper subsided. Consider, also, that during this time, there are a female child and the male child looking out of the window seeing all of this. This would give the female a superior relationship.

Now, also consider the tremendous emphasis on black female education. All through the South one can see, literally, a ten-to-one relationship between the education of the black male and the black female, at least up until World War II. The black male would quite often have to quit school to find a job and help the family out. The black female would continue in school. This would give her a superior position, education-wise, over the black male. That situation helped

5

to broaden the male-female gap further.

Consider what type of meaningful sexual relationship could there be between the black male and black female as a consequence. We can see how the young black female would continue to be competitive with and dominant over the young black male. This would give the young black male reasons to compete or fight with the black female rather than try to be superior. In this situation, we can see how the young unmarried black male, after impregnating the young black female, would have no conscious feelings about the consequent offspring of this sexual act. This may account for some of the marked increase in the number of illegitimate children in the black community.

What I am attempting to explain is that there is a competition between the young black male and the female for dominance, as in a competitive game. The reason is due to the background of superiority that has been artificially imposed upon the young black female because of the above-mentioned factors and others that I will allude to later.

There are factors that seem to go in a vicious circle in the relationship. There is the attitude of the black woman, who quite often is frigid because of the increased number of fibroids and consequent infections she has. In the home situation, because she is frigid, this gives her a superior attitude over the male, who quite often is constantly begging for sex and allowing the wife to make decisions, in the hope of attaining her sexual favors. We can envision a situation in which the female can coldly control the sexual situation to the point where she can become a tyrant, coldly detached from the sex needs because it only leads to frustration and further nervousness for her. This male-female relationship does not go unnoticed as far as the children are concerned. In any event, it seems like a vicious circle in the black community.

Some of the attitudes of the young black male toward the young black female can also be seen being programmed in his mind by the marked increase in broken homes in the black community. With an 80% divorce rate, we can hardly wonder at some of the attitudes of hate or competitiveness being engendered in children, both male and female, toward the opposite sex in these broken-home situations, thus perpetuating a vicious cycle of frustration in a society whose rules and laws are hostile.

During the practice of medicine, quite often one encounters a mother who brings in an impregnated unmarried daughter. As one impregnated young lady stated in front of her mother when the mother seemed to be shaken by the event, "How can you tell your mother that you have been having sexual intercourse?" This is true. How can a young girl tell her mother that she has had sexual relationships, particularly in the taboo type of background most black families have concerning sex. The most successful adjustments, other than the new legalized abortion that these relationships have brought about, have been attempts by the mother to embrace the young impregnated girl, as opposed to the other type parent who scolds, ridicules and sometimes punishes the young girl, who is very bewildered, to the point that she has nowhere to turn except back to her young lover, who is also immature.

This immaturity, coupled with the negative parental attitude, gives him the feeling, "well, if her mother and father don't want her, I shouldn't want her either." Quite often, the male has enough alibis from hearing the parents call the girl a "young whore," etc., to give him an excuse not to assume his paternal responsibilities. The young girl, who is really only a child, is literally left alone in this situation, and often the psychological scars on the young girl are worn for life.

On the other hand, parents who have embraced the young girl and helped her to solve this problem have not only helped the daughter but have helped the young man make satisfactory adjustments. In most of these instances the young man will marry the daughter, quite often gladly, because he becomes jealous of the attention heaped on the daughter and the unborn child by doting, impending grandparents.

A situation that I find most common in the black community, and in the young black female, is that the prettier young girls are often subjected to early sexual misfortunes. Of course, this often occurs more in situations in which both the mother and father are working, as in any lower economic class, and also in a crowded ghetto situation in which there are many social misfits who aren't "achievers" and who express their ego through sexual conquest of young girls. These male social misfits quite often use extreme persuasion and a multitude of tricks to get the younger girl to accept their advances and then proceed to blackmail her through sex until she finally becomes pregnant.

These situations change slightly in the middle-class black community. Unfortunately, there are few such communities when compared to the number of lower-class black communities. In the middle-class black, as well as the middle-class white, community there is more protection from the "bad boy" who needs ego trips through sexual conquests. Perhaps just as important, before legalized abortions, the middle class quite often could find a kind of medical professional who could help bring a late period "down" for certain considerations.

Now that we have legalized abortions, I think the middle class will avail themselves of the services more so than the

7

lower class, who are more religious and therefore less receptive to abortion. This will be a blow to the people who are involved with controlled population and birth control.

The other aspect of this chapter is whether "to have premarital sex" or not. I am not sure which is better. I have seen situations in which there has been considerable pre-marital sex, and much happiness has come from the relationship, even when there has been a considerable amount and variety of pre-marital sex. All in all, I feel it is an individual decision and that it is very important to know which is right for different individuals involved. However, I feel that the longer a female remains chaste, the better her chances are of selecting the individual of her choice, up to a certain point; particularly if she attends college. There are still men who feel that their wives and sisters, for some reason, are different from all other women on the face of the earth, and that they are all virtuous.

With better gynecological care for the black female and earlier and enlightened knowledge as to how to care for her body, the black female can have a monogamous, beautiful relationship, a situation that is almost completely dependent on her maintaining a completely healthy body, particularly in the pelvic area.

THE MENSTRUAL CYCLE

We will begin with a discussion of the menarche, the menstrual period which usually begins around ten to twelve years of age. The menstrual periods usually have a twenty-eight-day cycle. Day one of the period starts with the beginning of menses, which usually last from three to five days; then, there are twenty-three to twenty-five days of nonmenses. The fourteenth or fifteenth day is the midcycle from the beginning of menses. At this time, the ovary excretes an egg from its inner depths through its lining. This is the time when a woman is most susceptible to becoming pregnant. This egg comes up from the center of the ovary every month; the women produces approximately four hundred eggs during her lifetime fertility period. If she produces two eggs at the same time, and if they are fertilized by male sperm, she has fraternal twins. If, for some reason, the one egg is fertilized and divides, the woman develops identical twins.

The fertilization of an egg occurs by the sperm meeting the egg in the woman's Fallopian tube, one-third of the way from its outer edge. The tube is literally an extension of the womb and acts as a conduit for the egg until the egg reaches the uterus. This egg implants on the posterior superior aspect of the womb. If and when the sperm meets and penetrates the egg, fertilizes it, and is subsequently implanted on the uterine wall, then often a baby is born nine months later.

Ten to twelve days prior to ovulation, the body prepares the inner lining of the womb for reception of this fertilized egg. It is similar to what is seen in nature when birds prepare their nests for the hatching of eggs. When the egg does not become fertilized, there is no need for the increased blood vessels and increased sugar in the lining of the womb, and it literally sheds from the inside of the womb. This is the menses and the new start of a new cycle.

Needless to say, the most minimal time for conception is

within three to four days before the woman starts her menses and within three to four days after. The main reason that the woman begins pregnancy in her tubes is that male sperm, which is only 1/100 the size of the female egg, is able to get through fibrous infected bands, which are a sequel of tubal infections, to get to the egg and fertilize it two-thirds distance from the uterus. The fertilized egg--one hundred times larger than the sperm--may not be able to tread the route back to the womb that the sperm took to get to it, and it becomes entrapped in a mesh of infection and begins to grow in the tube, thus causing tubal pregnancy.

Many health-care people believe that increased pelvic inflammatory disease, (female organ infection), in black women is due to promiscuity. This is not usually true. There is a tremendous amount of disease among black women, most of it due to their propensity to form fibroids, whether due to the relatively long phallus of the black male and the subsequent trauma, keloid formation propensity of blacks, or the missionary way of sexual intercourse in individuals whose foreparents may have practiced sex with the female on top-- more practical in a hot climate. A relatively longer phallus and perhaps a more muscular introitus in the female may have developed. Subsequently, missionaries from a colder climate, who probably practiced intercourse in a male-on-top position because of the climate, imposed their method of sex position on black men with subsequent disasterous results for blacks.

I think that pelvic inflammations, endometriosis, and other diseases of black female organs are quite often due to the uterus not emptying properly of blood, trapped sperm, and cells that line the womb. Diseases of the female organs often result. All organs in the body must empty. I think that during menses, when the inside wall of the uterus is shedding, along with the blood vessels that help make up the spongy, nutritional tissue that has been built up to receive the fertilized ova, when the inside wall of the uterus does not receive the fertilized ova, it also sheds trapped sperm and discharge from the male genitalia. This shedding has to be unhampered and unencumbered by tampons or the uterus being in retroflexed position, e.g., not getting the benefits of gravity. The uterus has to be unencumbered by having a direct egress for the protein-rich, carbohydrate-rich tissue as menstrum to leave the uterus easily; indeed, to leave the vagina easily. When this tissue does not have free egress, it putrifies, causing a culture media in which bacteria can multiply freely. The culture-media material is called menstrum: menstrum used in the laboratory commercially to grow bacteria. A "stopping up" of this rich, infectious-prone uterine material causes putrification and a considerable amount of growth and mutation of the woman's own harmless

bacteria, particularly from the adjacent anus, into a very
virulent destructive bacteria. The change of virulence of
bacteria that are indigenous to an area happens to all body
organs in which inadequately opened orifices hamper the normal egress of body secretions--whether they are sinuses in
sinusitis, lungs in pneumonia, bladders in cystitis, kidneys
in pyelonephrosis, and certainly, the uterus in endometritis.
It is from this endometritis--inflammation of the uterine
wall--caused by the inability of the uterus to empty itself
adequately, particularly during the menstrual cycle--that
an infection develops that spreads to the Fallopian tubes and
other female glands.

If coitus is performed during this time, inflammation
goes into the male, the prostate gland in particular, which
acts as a reservoir of repeated infections, particularly for
the female during sexual acts. It is this reservoir from the
male and from the female tubes, Bartholin glands, etc., that
causes great consternation in the black community. With the
first sign of pus in the male or female, some married people
believe that his or her spouse has been "playing around," when
actually this has not necessarily been true. Local infections, however, often occur and are difficult to clear up,
particularly if the infection becomes chronic. This suspicion of infidelity causes a lot of grief in the black community. This will be detailed later.

THE PHYSICAL ANATOMY OF SEX

An understanding of Darwin's Theory will be helpful
here. There is an interesting aspect to the physical anatomy
of the sexes, when we take into consideration the comparative
anatomy between man and other mammals, particularly as it
concerns the female uterus. The anatomic position of the
uterus is anteflexed or forward; the round ligaments, which
are two rope-like structures on the sides of the top of the
uterus, pull the large top part of the uterus forward.

Let us assume that we, both blacks and whites, are de-
scendants of the lower mammals. Since these mammals are quadrupeds, the uterus in these animals, aided by the pull of
gravity, would normally be anteflexed or pushed toward the anterior wall of the abdominal cavity. Consider the human female, who has assumed an erect position. The uterus is strained
to remain in an anteflexed or anterior position. This anatomic position is inherited from our lower ancestors, who are
quadrupeds. Assume, also, that the female, in addition to
standing erect, which places a strain on the round ligaments
to hold the large fundus forward, has the problem compounded
by being "fashionable:" wearing high-heeled shoes, which tilt
the pelvis even more. Further, if the female sleeps on her
back, her body is in a 180-degree angle from her basic anatomic position as a descendant of the lower mammals who sleep
in a prone or face-down position, on all fours. Considering
this, we can see how the large part of the uterus or fundus
might be subjected to falling into an unnatural position, or
retroflexed position, by the pull of gravity. Consider further
instances in which males in the act of intercourse enter in a
face-to-face position with the male on top. This further im-
poses a hardship on the round ligaments that help hold the
heavy part of the womb up and forward to keep the uterus in
its normal position, particularly if the male uses the method
of tilting the female pelvis. And most especially if the female has a large postpartum uterus, which, in most instances,

is not given the six-week involution period by the male partner before resuming sex.

According to "barber shop" sources, the man-on-top face-to-face, or "missionary" way is not the way Africans practiced intercourse before the missionaries landed. The reason the white man practiced it the way he did was probably overlooked. We can see how much more comfortable or cooler it would be in a hot climate to practice intercourse with the male in the rear or side-by-side or the more fragile female on top; whereas, in cold climates, it would probably be more comfortable to practice it in a face-to-face position with the male on top as the white missionaries did. This preference could account for some relative differences in the size and length of the phallus and the vagina; it may also account for differences in size of the internal genital organs. Certainly, it is not inconceivable that a longer black phallus may have been a by-product of this side-by-side, female on top, or posterior approach; for we can easily imagine a certain loss of functioning length of the phallus by position alone in the non-missionary way. There would also be a certain propensity of the female, whose pubococcygeus muscle and vaginal muscles were developed to a high degree to hold the thrusting head more firmly, to encourage and increase in length by the "adaptive process" the male phallus and decrease in size the female's vagina and/or pelvic outlet over a period of millions of years with a "cool way" of practicing intercourse. Other factors which may account for this smaller black pelvis, will be described later.

Intercourse from the rear, side, or with the female on top would allow the normally small vagina of the black female to accommodate better the relatively long phallus of the black male. These positions would keep the relatively large fundus of the black female's uterus punched forward and would more easily drain infection and stagnation of uterine secretions--in an African setting.

Perhaps this position was practiced before the missionaries arrived. Missionaries who had probably practiced sex with the male on top, which was more desirable in a cold climate where individuals were also in a relatively naked situation. As with the skin color and the hair texture, genetics enabled certain physical attributes to survive as an adaptation to better propagate the species in relation to the environment, which, at that time, was the strongest force controlling man's survival.

As a corollary that will be covered later, the size and shape of the white male's phallus and white female's vagina may have been determined by their environment, also.

In the pre-missionary position, the black phallus acts to keep the fundus anteflexed and empty of menstrum; discharge is very easy in that position. In the missionary position, the black male actually helps develop retroflexion, and stagnation, of the uterine discharges and chronic infections in the black female.

The large muscular black female uterus may be a by-product of the black males' and black females' tapered hips, an enhancement for fast mobility in an environment where several types of carnivorous wild animals could devour the slow wide-hipped male or female. With the narrow anthropoid hip, the uterus had to develop a large muscular fundus to push the black baby's head out.

To fully appreciate the development of the anthropoid pelvis, we also have to reflect on our ancestors, who were not clothed or were sparsely clothed, if we are to keep in perspective the full meaning of the female pelvis development. I think that in the development of the black female, the thighs are proportionally larger than the calves in contrast to the white female, and the hips are somewhat streamlined, perhaps more than any other group of females.

This may be due to the fact that in a warm climate the people wear little clothing or none. We can see how the male could be attracted to the smooth thin lines of the black female's pelvis and hips. Because of this, it is possible that she could be subjected to more breeding over the years. This race would have females with small calves and very beautiful thighs. Thus, the black female with an anthropoid-type pelvis evolved. The white female with the gynecoid-type pelvis was in a cold climate, and usually wore full-bodied clothes; she could only expose her calves to the suitor. This may account for the larger, streamlined, beautiful calves of the white female. However, the size and shape of the hips and thighs of both races may be an architectural by-product of the pelvis. The wider hips, or gynecoid-type pelvis, of the white female allows a basic ease of childbirth that may have been a by-product of her environment, or may have been the prime reason for her physiognomy as well as the white male's physiognomy, the large calves are an architectural by-product. Anthropoid-type pelvis or hips of the black female are much narrower from side-to-side as compared to white females. In a warm climate, where the black females were not subjected to the coldness, pneumonia, etc., there may have been a tendency to have this type of anthropoid pelvis perpetuated in the black race, according to Darwinian reasoning. Also, the black female's thighs and hips are probably a by-product of male development and need for a body structure that could move fast in an animal-infested environment such as Africa.

White women, having a small uterus, have very few problems with the retroflexion of the uterus; the uterus is so small that it empties menstrum, etc., easily. Because of this

15

they have fewer problems with pelvic inflammation than black
females. Black women, having a large fundus of the uterus,
are more prone to fibroids and retroflexion, and more infection than white females. We should also be aware that the
black male is perhaps overly endowed and may be rough with the
black female's sex organs, thus causing more inflammation because of the trauma to her organs. Perhaps we practice sex
like whites, which may not be our natural position.

Why does the black woman have so many tumors and fibroids?
One cause is due to the excessive length of the male phallus,
relatively; it pulverizes the internal organs of the female,
pushing the uterus against the back of the pelvis traumatically
during the act of intercourse, when practiced the missionary
way. It is this traumatic battering of the female organs
that causes hemorrhage and, literally, a picture of a beaten
steak in the female uterus when the male is finished with sexual intercourse. This type of inflammation leads to fibrous
degeneration, particularly in individuals who are prone to
having large scars or keloids, etc.--for example, black women
and men.

The relative excessive length of the black male phallus
compensates for the marked reduction of available phallus that
finally reaches the female vagina in the non-missionary position. There may be many reasons why the non-missionary position of intercourse was better for Africans, but we should
think of situations in which the African people may have lived
in an excessively hot climate in which body contact may have
been held to a minimum during the sex act.

In any event, I think black males and females, for their
own health's sake, should revert to this non-missionary form
of intercourse. As I will explain later, in addition to the
fibroids and the subsequent retroflexion of the top of the
uterus, retained secretions, and subsequent chronic infections,
we can see how this would lead to many other diseases in the
black female and the male. By having intercourse in the
"non-missionary" way, the black male's phallus could act as
a perpetual lever to keep the top of the uterus punched for-
ward--an absolute necessity to reduce infection, frigidity,
etc.

Not the least cause of this easy retroflexion of the
black female uterus is its excessive size and the excessive
room posteriorly in the black female's antropoid-type pelvis,
which allows the fundus to fall back easily into the hollow
of the sacrum. The large fundus of the black uterus may be a
compensatory mechanism as a consequence of the narrow hips,
to better push the head of the black fetus out during delivery.
The "molding" of the black fetus head is a normal by-product
of this small outlet. Retroflexion of the uterus can be due
to the abnormal high angle of the male phallus, particularly

if he has the legs of the woman on top of him while performing with the male on top. The phallus rides on the top of the uterus where the angle of the entrance helps push it backward.

The male's prostate is filled with pus when he has regular intercourse with an infected female. This, in turn, causes a considerable amount of inflammatory fibrous-type nodules similar to what one sees in the black female's uterus. This, of course, leads to a reduction in hormone production necessary to make the man potent, and also causes obstruction of the urine, which can lead to hypertension in the black male. Of course, prostatic operations remove these nodules in the black male.

Cancer of the prostate is another risk for the black male having intercourse with an infected female. The sad part of this vicious cycle is that the woman often incurs the disease from a nonsexual situation: a hard or closely repeated child birth; not allowing complete involution of her internal organs after child birth and before resuming sex; the large "boggy" uterus falls or is pushed backward during the post-partum period; poor anal wiping techniques, wearing of tampons, infected abortion, etc. Perhaps at fault as much, or more than anything else, is the delay in seeking competent medical help, for her mind has been programmed to believe that her condition is of veneral origin; she or her husband has been unfaithful. Unfortunately, in many cases, uninformed medical people, neighbors, etc., have only confused the situation more for the young black couple.

The body, being as beautiful as it is, especially in the area of pus formation, whether it is an abscess under the skin or an abscess anywhere, immediately sends soldiers, that is, white cells and other humoral agents, to localize these infected areas; that is, fight organisms, for example, entercoccis, E. coli, staphylococcus, etc., and in time it will form a fibrous wall around this infection, similar to the formation of spider webs by the spider. Then it will send other humoral agents into the center of the abscesses that have been walled off and in time destroy these invaders. Thus it turns into a hydrosalpinx in which water forms in the tubes from the previous abscess or pyosalpinx.

This becomes a chronic process, and any disease that becomes chronic becomes almost impossible to heal. This is where the difficulty arises in the healing of these women by temporary expedients, which most of the time is a little vaginal cream and a couple of shots of penicillin, which may heal early acute processes but not the chronic ones.

Actually, the pathology is much deeper. It requires prolonged treatment and perhaps a correction of the abnormally positioned organs by suspension of the uterus and the tubes and/or insertion of pessaries of the gyneflod or Smith-Hodge

variety. It requires a change in position of sex by the black
male. When infection is present, the male should protect
himself by a diaphragm or a condom from the massive pelvic
discharge that ensues from the unwielding head of the phallus,
which ruptures the pyosalpinx (abscesses) and forces the pus
medially through the uterus, out of the cervix, and into his
internal glands, particularly the prostate. There it lies
dormant and allows the "bacteria" to nurture themselves and
often undergo mutation within the male organ into other more
virulent forms of organisms which will be shot back into the
woman's internal organs, which are now unprotected from this
"new" invader because the female's body may not now recognize
some of her own germs, germs which may return in a more virulent form, and they do return to the female, who is literally
a "waste basket" for the male's discharge. There is, therefore, little wonder why, at times, I tell the infected couple
that it would take a "Philadelphia lawyer" to unscramble the
mess.

But more important, particularly for the black couple in
this situation, is the social and economic disaster that often comes about when well-meaning and very honest "advisors"
and even physicians, innocently or otherwise, tell one of the
spouses or both that there has been some philandering when in
most instances, particularly for the blacks, this has not
necessarily been the case.

More importantly, particularly from the black female's
point of view, economically and socially, she will often not
seek medical help because of her fear that she will be ostra-
cized by the attending physician, nurses, and other paramedics,
who will "look down their noses" at her or, more seriously,
contact her husband or paramour, particularly through zealous
and often honest, but unfortunately not knowledgeable, public
health officials...officials who may blame her for the infection or insinuate that she is not clean or that she is promiscuous. She will, therefore, not seek help until the last
minute, until the burning, the foul odor, and the pain literally destroy her. Of course, everyone around her will be
affected like the concentric circles which appear after a
rock is thrown into water--her husband, her children, her
unborn children's children, etc.

Treatment should be undertaken over a protracted period
of time, with other adjuvant treatments such as sitz baths
and deep sound and heat to the pelvic organs, etc., coupled
with instructions on hygiene, sex-position practices, as well
as the nonobstruction of the menstrual flow by tampons, etc.
If these precautions are not taken completely, the black female will soon be back in the doctor's office with complaints
similar to those she had before.

One of the tragic problems here is the conversation

that goes on, between the black woman and her husband, which
I have alluded to earlier. The black woman becomes extremely
frustrated and frigid and may say "All you want out of me is
my body". The black man may respond, "If I'm not doing it,
somebody else is," and this makes the black woman even angrier
toward the black male. It gets to the point where she screams
from these false accusations. At the least, it leads to a
most difficult situation, particularly with a black female who
has a vaginal discharge and can't find any answer other than
believing her husband has been unfaithful. In most instances,
this is not true; often, he is not the source of her female
infection. Often it comes from her own anus, or from towels
she has used to wash her face when she has had a cold, or
from pyogenic bacteria that lodge in the genital organs
and take hold easily when the organs are abnormally positioned
and their normal rich discharge is obstructed thereby allowing
these relatively safe organisms to undergo mutation and become highly virulent.

Oral sex is perhaps becoming more popular with married
blacks than previously, particularly with surrounding facili-
ties becoming more hygenic. Here, too, the individuals who
participate in oral sex quite often are those who had a previous sex problem, for the "little climaxes" received by the
female in oral sex cannot possibly match the "maximal" climax
of normal sex.

Often the woman becomes more ill, for not only is the
mouth spreading foreign bacteria into a closed area, where
they incubate and destroy the normal vaginal flora, but the
woman who does not subsequently practice normal sex and reach
a "maximal climax" will often have her turbinates engorged,
will remain in a protracted state of excitement, and, if
continued, will stay in a state of nervous exhaustion and
agitation by the repeated small "hot flashes" brought on by
the unfinished or unfulfilled eroticism of oral sex. It is
a vicious circle.

Practicing anal intercourse with vaginal intercourse has
a similar effect on the female's vaginal flora; like oral sex,
it causes some of the worst cases of salpingitis. Wiping the
anus wrong, not douching after sex, etc., are some other
simple but poor hygienic measures that can cause refractive
salpingitis and thus affect the whole life not only of the
mother and father but also of yet unborn generations of
blacks.

The woman seems to act as a waste basket for the discharge of the man with whom she is having sex, particularly
if she is extremely tight and agile in her act. In this way,
she will, of course, receive more discharge into her internal
organs. If it is an older man, there is a great possibility
that it might be the discharge of pus received from several

19

women. If the girl is young, she will wind up with a uterus
full of infection, and if she is not extremely careful, this
infection will continue all of her life, even to the point
that her tubes will close, and she will never be able to become impregnated, particularly if her organs are out of place.

Every individual on earth has his or her own bacteria
that inhabits his glands, skin, and entire body. If a woman
has just one sexual partner, usually her body, by receiving
his discharge, and his bacteria, can produce humoral agents
in time to counter his discharge and his bacteria. If,
however, she has contact with too many men over too short a
time, there is no way that her body can counter the on-
slaught of so many different bacteria, and she will become
infected particularly if her organs are displaced or in any
way physically abnormal.

With the wider anterior posterior dimension of the black
female pelvis, it would also seem easier for her uterus to
fall backward into the hollow of the sacrum. When performing
hysterectomies on some black females, I am at times amazed at
how deep I have to dissect. This is in contrast to the narrower anterior posterior width of the white female's pelvis,
which makes it more difficult for the uterus to fall backward and become retroflexed. This is quite often the catalyst of the whole infection controversy, uterine retroflexion.

There may be more than a casual relationship, within
certain time limits, between climax and ovulation and subsequent pregnancy in humans, similar to what is seen in lower
animals. Climax may be a stimulus to ovulation in humans
during their period of estrus or "heat"--as noted by clini-
cal temperature elevation during certain times of the month.
Often the woman knows "the moment she gets pregnant." Nature seems to have provided a built-in birth control mechanism
for the animals on earth. Not only are there changes that
come about with age, to reduce the population, in both the
female and the male--arthritis, arterioscleroses, heart
disease, etc., but there are also changes in the female
sexual and reproductive structures with each pregnancy that
work against subsequent pregnancies, e.g., the stretching of
the ligaments holding the female organs in place. In both
the black and white female, the bladder lowers into the vagina to form a pouch where urine is trapped, becomes stagnant,
and infects the whole genito-urinary tract, to say nothing
of the reduction in ecstasy when the trapped old urine empties
onto the male as he inserts his phallus into the vagina to
initiate the act, or to the continuous urination on him all
during the act because of loss of sphincteric control by the
female. Whatever effect it has on the male, it literally
"blows the female's mind." Not only does she have to worry
about the hygienic and ecstatic effect, but she can in no way

reach a climax because she can't relax all during the act.
She is consciously trying to hold her sphincter closed. No
relaxation, no climax, in time--frigidity. With frigidity,
there is a reduction in the number of sexual contacts, thus
reduced pregnancies.

Likewise, frigidity for the black female is also a consequence of repeated pregnancies, particularly if they are not
spaced relatively far apart. There is stretching of the round
ligaments, retroflexion of the uterus into the deep hollow
recess of the black pelvis and the consequent chronic infection, tumors, discharge, etc. In both instances, the black
woman and the white woman, changes occur in their personality,
their skin, vaginal mucous membrane, etc. Even if changes
occurred only in the genital organs, the couple could probably
make it, but the anxiety and bickering from the frustrations
of no climax for months and years almost invariably leads to
divorce and reduced baby production.

The ultimate assault for the female, and the male, is
when both ovaries are removed, for after that there is almost
always divorce. It is most often in the middle of the couple's
life and the act of sex is not usually that important. However, when the ovaries are removed, there is not only an
aversion to sex by the female--she actually hates it--but
there is also considerable frustration and anxiety towards
the whole male. This constant bickering in turn has an effect
on the male. For when a woman's ovaries are present there
seems to be a hormone emanating from her smell, the taste of
her nipples, etc., that stimulates eroticism, etc. This
latter is usually gone after castration, and divorce is often
inevitable.

It is my opinion that early repair of cystocaeles,
urethrocaeles, retroflexion of the uterus, early hysterectomies without oophorectomy would do much to reduce the large
number of divorces, and misunderstandings leading to divorce
that often go on for years prior to the divorce.

All during marriage there are physiological as well as
pathological causes of reduction in ovarian function because
of reduction in sexual contact and subsequent climaxing.
Such as, for a time after the baby is born, absence of partners from each other, e.g., illness of the male or female as
a physiological cause. Fibroids, tumors, bouts of salpingitis,
retroflexion of the uterus are examples of pathological causes
for reduction of ovarian function and it is during these times
that "changes" occur in the female, indistinguishable from
those that occur after surgical menopause: irritableness,
"hot flashes", etc. It is during these times that often the
seed of a marital dissolution is planted. Often irrevocably
so.

This can account for the almost sure doom of second

marriages, for the woman carries into the second marriage the cystocaeles, fibroids, salpingitis, etc., that made her first marriage a "bomb." The man, of course, carries into the second marriage the alcoholism, the bad work record, the support payments, etc. All these things, coupled with the markedly complex relationships with children of others, the reduced choices of selection, the aging of the partners, who for the most part, are "set in their ways" usually winds up with a second marriage with ten times the problems of the first marriage and when they do make it, it is because the partners are often too proud to acknowledge failure and hang on in spite of the much more severe hardships encountered during their first marriage. Of course, with multiple marriages it would seem an arithmetical impossibility for tranquility. It's like buying a used car.

Incidentally, just as a woman goes through changes in her skin--acne, her nervous system--anxiety, her cardiovascular system--arrythmias and tachycardia--her vaginal mucosa, etc., when she lacks ovarian function, there are changes that occur when her ovaries are functioning healthily. Tranquility, smooth face, hair stops falling out, but, as much as anything, there seems to be an ecstatic odor emanating from her as well as an erotic taste to her skin and her nipples that usually makes her super attractive even to men she never realized could be interested--a real pied piper she becomes.

THE PHYSIOPATHOLOGY OF SEX

Black women are seriously hampered in receiving medical
care because, in most instances, medical rules for white women are followed and insisted upon in Western society, for
they are what all medical men are taught in this white-
dominated society. Thus, the black population has to shoulder
another burden in its attempt to be treated in a society that
gauges all females by the white female's anatomy. How is this
important? I think many pelvic inflammations, endometrioses,
and other diseases of the black female organs are basically
due to the fact that the uterus does not empty properly at all
times, not because of gonorrhea or promiscuity which is taught
and believed by some doctors, black and white, all of whom are
oriented to and have adapted to the white concept of medicine
in the hope of passing the requirements to practice medicine.
The prime diseases of the black female sex organs are a consequence of this; all organs in the body must empty. I would
think that during the menses, the inside cellular wall of the
uterus is shedding along with the blood vessels, which helps
make up the spongy, sweet tissue that has been built up to
receive the fertilized ova, along with trapped sperm and discharge from the male genitalia. This shedding has to be unencumbered by situations such as the uterus being in an unnatural position and, therefore, not getting the benefits of
gravity and also absorbing material in the vagina, which
hampers its complete discharge from the body. Menstrum has to
be easily discharged by having direct egress. The protein-
rich, carbohydrate-rich material has to leave the uterus
easily; for menstrum is the most fertile of all tissue for
growing bacteria. When it does not empty easily, it becomes
an ideal bacterial culture media. The material, menstrum, is
used in laboratories commercially to grow bacteria. A setting
up of this rich infectious-prone material in the retroflexed
uterus, where it putrefies, causes a considerable amount of
growth and mutation of the individual's own bacteria into a

23

very virulent bacteria, which acts to destroy the individual
itself. This bacterial-caused destruction occurs in all other
organs of the body and their secretions when they are obstructed, certainly in the uterus where endometritis develops. It
is this retroflexion, that causes the inability of the uterus,
particularly during the menstrual cycle, to empty itself
adequately, and sets up infection that goes to the tubes, the
Bartholin glands, the Nabothian glands, and other female glands.
If coitus is performed during this time of infection, infection enters the organ of the male, particularly the prostate.
The prostate acts as a reservoir of repeated infections,
infections that go back and forth from the male to the female
and often appear to be veneral in nature. The muscle around
the prostate contracts during ejaculation, shooting the infection into the female's internal organs. It is this reservoir from the male and from the female tubes and glands that
causes considerable consternation in the black community.
With the first sign of pus in the male or female, some sex
partners may believe that his or her special partner has been
"playing around" on the other partner when this has not
necessarily been true. Often, it has come from the infected
areas, which are extremely difficult to clear up once the
infection has become chronic. This suspicion of infidelity,
coupled with the usually associated female frigidity in the
infection circle, precipitates fights and shootings that cause
more grief in the black community.

Often, black women are reluctant to go to physicians,
black or white, for almost all are programmed white and believe that the infected woman is almost always unfaithful or
filthy and at times express this belief to the woman and or her
spouse only to have it "blow her or his mind," particularly if
she has had only one sex partner. If a culture of the discharge were done, it would, in most instances, show that the
woman has been infected by her own discharge from her infected
tonsils, teeth, or in most instances from E. coli or enterococcus bacteria, whose normal habitat, in most instances, is
less than one inch away--the anus. Incidentally, it is the
repeated chronic infection in the male that leads to surgical
procedure, such as a prostatectomy, usually when the male
reaches his late fifties or early sixties. Quite often it
is due to intercourse with women who have had a chronic infection, particularly if the man has contracted gonorrhea and
did not get proper treatment in the acute phase during his
younger years. Gonorrhea, of course, lasts only a few days,
but it breaks down areas for other non-venereal bacteria to
come in and "set up house." However, other non-venereal diseases are almost as bad. Long-term antibiotics, massage of
the prostate gland, or as the old kings and the other nobles
once did, have intercourse with extremely young females, will

incite a more powerful contraction of the muscle surrounding the prostate at the expense of discharging "pus" at climax into the belly of the young female, thus allowing his parenchymal prostatic tissue to re-grow and produce sex hormones. The result is a revitalization or rejuvenation of the youth of the older man. This may account for the fact that older men look younger when married to younger women, and the younger women look older. In any event, there seems to be an inarguable attraction of the older man for the younger woman.

Modern society has imposed a situation in which young females will fill their vagina with absorbing material to keep from having to get off the production line or not allow menstrual discharge into the vaginal reservoir. Consequently, she sets up a potential situation for stagnation of the menstrum in the uterus. Here, again, this is particularly bad for black females, whose small muscular vaginal orifices are not suited for this. We can compare the situation of filling the bladder, the kidney reservoir, with material that impedes the minute-to-minute emptying of the kidneys. If this happens, the individual will develop pyelonephritis as a consequence; or if one blocked the rectum, a reservoir for feces; or blocked the nose, which is a reservoir for sinuses and eye drainage; or the eustachian tubes, for ear drainage. The consequences to the main organ would be the same, infection. As mentioned previously, white women, having a small uterus, have very few problems with retroflexion of the uterus. Their uterus is so small that quite often it empties easily, and they have fewer problems with pelvic inflammation. We must be aware of the fact that blacks have a large fundus of the uterus, which causes them to be more prone to fibroids and more uterine obstruction and fallopian discharge and consequent retroflexion and infection. One should be aware that the black penis is perhaps overly long and quite rough on the black female's small vagina and that they practice sex like whites. Because of the angle of entrance, it pushes the heavy fundus backward stretching the fragile small round ligaments, particularly in the immediate postpartum state or where large tumors in the fundus help tip the uterus backward. The black female is often suffering with some inflammation because of this. It is a vicious circle and often the young black infected female will present herself to the doctors, complaining of "menstrual cramp" or backache--the two most frequent complaints when a woman has a retroflexed uterus--although the woman may be virginal.

I firmly believe that in the act of coitus the complete and total deep penetration of the available phallus into the depth of the vagina is the only way that a woman can reach a total climax. Fibroid tumors cause a considerable amount of pelvic inflammation in the black female. Because of her large uterus and small vagina, she is prone to have a considerable amount of retroflexion and subsequent stagnation of menstrual discharge and inflammation. This, of course, will lead to frigidity. As the young black married male begins to have intercourse, after the first baby or two, usually he will come home to a wife who has a big uterus, which is retroflexed; therefore, she usually has salpingitis. In order to reach a successful climax, the woman has to be totally relaxed to allow the total penetration by the available male phallus. If the female is not totally relaxed, there is no way she can reach her climax. I cannot help but feel that the ability to reach a climax regularly comes from previous easy climaxes because of the conditioning and anticipation in the female with the healthy pelvis. It may play a significant role in conception because often at surgery the infertile female with occluded tubes or salpingitis has ovaries covered with cysts that I believe are a consequence of unruptured Graafian follicles or unruptured ova or eggs and numerous bouts of almost climaxing. Women who have little or no pathology often have smooth ovaries and characteristic wounds in them from ruptured Graafian follicles, a consequence of the ability of the healthy woman to climax and consequently to become simultaneously impregnated. But more on this later.

One also has to recognize that a female's vagina is approximately three inches in length and that the phallus may be from six to ten inches in length when erection occurs, and even longer at the height of coitus, just before ejaculation. We should recognize that each thrust of the phallus probably pushes the whole internal organs four to six inches upward into the internal areas of the female. This, of course, means that the uterus, tubes, and ovaries can be subjected to considerable batting around in the pelvis, which, if infected, will give the female pain, and the disease can cause considerable problems. The infected female reflexively knows that if she relaxes completely, allowing the male to penetrate her to the fullest extent of his phallus, the man will hurt her. We can imagine what would happen to abscessed tubes that are pushed one-half a foot into the female's belly as the male becomes aggressive and, indeed, rough as he approaches his climax and pushes against the cervix of the uterus at that moment. Surely, the inflamed tubes and the surrounding small bowel become irritated even more. Usually, the body has corralled the pus and infection into a small area at the end of the tube called a pyosalpinx. The tube, which has the purulent material, may burst open by the enlarged hard phallus pinning the abscess against the back of the pelvis and causing a momentary reopening of the distal end of the abscessed tube. Localized peritonitis ensues. This, of course, causes

ileus or paralytic bowel obstruction and subsequent piling up
of gas and stagnation in the female's intestine for several
days after intercourse. Everything she eats causes "gas."
The small bowel becomes paralyzed; ingested food subsequently
becomes stagnated in the intestine. "Gas" is increased in the
stagnated food, and a long chain of uncomfortable situations
develop for the female with pelvic inflammation after intercourse, conditioning her mind adversely to the sex act. In
order to protect herself subsequently, the black female will
tighten up and guard herself with thighs, fingernails, etc.,
against this excess penetration, which is usually ecstatic for
normal women. Meanwhile, even before she can "get herself
together," the male is on her again; the same thing is repeated. Soon the "patient's" mind becomes "conditioned"
like in Pavlov's experiments; as the thrusting phallus pounds
into her, there is a direct relationship between the distance
she allows it to go into her and the amount of misery that
she suffers afterward. Instead of concentrating on total
relaxation necessary for climax, total removal of the dampening
effect of the cerebral cortex on the lower brain centers, I
feel that this is absolute, the female has to become completely
decorticate in order to reach total climax or total relaxation;
the latter, of course, is a prerequisite for the former. So,
instead of this becoming a subcorticate and perhaps subcerebrate thing, as is necessary to reach a climax, the woman
has to continue to manifest a corticate situation. She cannot
revert to a subcerebrate or subcorticate state, for she is afraid of getting hurt by the enlarging male phallus approaching
climax, so she closes her eyes, shifts her hips and tries to
relax, but she cannot.

There seems to be a climax center below the cerebrum
level in the brain that is triggered when the penis pushes to
the depth of the normal female organs and pushes the female
pelvic organs against a trigger mechanism in the back of the
pelvis, which may be the pelvic nerve plexus of Frankenhausern.
This climax mechanism, I believe, causes the release of stored-
up energy and hormones, etc., in several of the body's systems.
It seems like a symphonic concert where the woman has to reach
her climax on "cue" from the man or vice versa. In any event,
as the woman approaches climax, she must be able to totally
relax, to open her legs as wide as possible to allow total
penetration by the available male phallus. At climax there is
a heat that comes over the woman, giving impetus to the male's
release. All of this has to come about in split-second se-
quences. The pelvically-inflamed woman tries to open her legs
widely for this split-second happening, but she cannot because
previous nights at relaxation and allowing too much penetration
have caused her protracted pain for several days, and her mind
is conditioned against this. The magic second passes, and the

27

distracted female with pelvic inflammation does not climax. She lays there all "hot and bothered" like after a super "petting session." Finally, if the inability to reach a climax is repeated over and over again, the female's mind and body become conditioned to the fact that just before the male climax, when he usually becomes extremely rough and his muscles tighten, a cue for the female to allow her mind to totally relax as control goes from the cerebrum to the lower brain centers which automatically take over, such as in the respiratory or cardiac centers, and allows her to reach a climax. But because her mind is conditioned, she tightens herself up, making it impossible for her to reach a climax. The female has a "bad trip" and she is usually still quite excited and unfulfilled after the male has finished. The female cannot sleep restfully until four or five o'clock in the morning when she cools off naturally; then she has to assume her responsibilities with the children or her job after only a couple of hours sleep, day in and day out. This makes her extremely agitated over a period of time. The healthy pelvic woman does become decerebrate, I think, at the moment of climax, regardless of her station in life, she acts like an animal when true climax is reached.

The healthy woman can relax completely, and you can tell this because she will open her legs wide and pull the man into her so that she gets the maximum penetration of the available phallus to hit the nervous plexus that causes her to climax. When this relaxation cannot come about, it affects not only the immediate female organs, but it affects the female's whole body and mind. It affects her sinuses, lungs, skin, etc. The female, after a successful climax, is able to turn over and sleep, relax, and be tranquil. This is very necessary, particularly in today's world, where there is so much stress on each individual that tranquility is necessary. The lack of sexual tranquilization may account for the marked increase in the use of pills and alcohol, which I will cover in more detail later. The female who does not climax is usually bothered the next night or so by the male, for there seems to be an unfulfillment of both, and although the male will climax, it will not be maximal for him.

The following night or so, the infected female will let out invidious remarks, such as "that's all you want to do," and the male will continue to play with her until she becomes excited to have intercourse again. When the inflamed female has intercourse this time, she goes through the same thing, thinking it might be a little better than it was before. She closes her eyes, shifts her pelvis, etc., hoping that the phallus will not hit the "sore spot." But the same thing happens again, and the female ends up more frustrated than ever and unable to sleep. She is even more tired and nervous

than before. Soon you will find the two people making in-
sinuations and arguing over incidental things; the female
saying, "All you want is my body." "You are not going to kill
me." "You don't love me," etc. The man accuses her of infidelity, saying, "If I ain't getting it, someone else is."
The woman knows this is far from the truth. She has no desire
for any male. Indeed, she becomes quite frigid. In many
of these cases, the female at four or five o'clock in the
morning lies beside a fairly well-satisfied male, who has
"rolled" off her and fallen immediately to sleep. In any event,
the woman gets only one or two hours of sleep. Imagine this
happening every night for a week or two or for several years.
Usually, at the end of that time, the woman will turn into a
nervous wreck and seek nerve pills from anyone. On the other
hand, the black male in the above situation will more often
than not be refused, for it is really "killing" his wife.

In fact, I would dare to say that a lot of the husbands
will say to the female, "Take this money and go to the doctor
and let him fix you up." The black female will go into the
hospital to rest and be treated for a couple of weeks, where
she will wonder why she is not like other women. Then, after
two weeks of rest in the hospital, the female will go back to
her husband with the best of intentions to be a good partner
to him. But after two or three bouts of the roughness that
the black man is known for, the female is "down in her stomach
again," and the situation is repeated. This is particularly
true if the original pathology is not corrected. Soon the
black male has either become an alcoholic, drug addict, or
has found another woman. Unfortunately, social economics play
a role here. Those who cannot afford to take pills, alcohol,
or dope find that in our economic system it is impossible to
support two women. Divorce results, and the black child
suffers. The whole situation puts the black man socially and
economically at a tremendous disadvantage with almost all
other races. A male child, in particular, is most difficult
to raise without a father image. I believe that the black
female subconsciously encourages the black male to go have an
affair, yet hoping that he will continue to be the father of
her children and the head of the household, which is really
all she wants at this stage. I believe that this may be a
reversion to her natural African polygamous way of sharing
her spouse. Sometimes the black male gets caught up in the
white man's rules and the "other woman" constantly puts pressure on him to either "defecate or get off the pot." Unfortunately, he has to look at it objectively. He has a
certain amount of money; he can take care of only one woman
in Western society. Therefore, he has to get rid of wife
number one. Of course, this is against his basic African
and new American culture, to a certain extent. It only leads

to confusion on his part, and divorce. It leads to a whole
new generation of children without fathers, adds further confusion and further debilitates the black race. In Africa,
or where polygamy is practiced, which is our natural culture,
the man can choose wife number two when wife number one is
not able to have sex regularly, and the household continues
serenely and without interruption. However, the black woman
in America thinks like the white woman, although her body is
basically African.

The black female becomes adamant about her stand, such as,
"He has done me wrong," etc., and she goes to the courts for
divorce, or she resorts to her own method of handling the
situation, the knife or pistol. It puts us in a real bind in
this white man's world.

On the other hand, the white woman usually has relatively
little problems with her uterus because it is small, anteflexed, and quite often without tubal abscesses; with her
wide pelvis, she does not have the problems that the black
woman has, and can almost always fulfill the sexual needs of
her man. The white man's problems, if and when they occur,
are usually not sexual. This is a tremendous advantage for
him in the day-to-day competition for a living, particularly
when all of the rules favor him.

The black man, who is a muscular individual, not only
because he is from a muscular area but because of certain
selective breeding during slavery, usually vents his frustration with alcohol or drugs or even by "sneaking around" with
some other man's wife. Recently, the black man has been able
to take advantage of "A.D.C." mothers. Perhaps even a
different situation is that he is enjoying more access to the
white woman. I believe that there is more than a casual
relationship between the increased number of black men and white
women relationships. Usually, the black man is able to ob-
tain more sex from the white woman. Because of this, I feel
that the black man and the white woman are usually attracted
to each other. The white man, of course, has always been
extremely attracted to the black woman. This probably accounts, to a great extent, for our continued survival in this
foreign-to-us situation, although there are certain physical
problems making that type of relationship almost impossible
where child bearing is a consequence because of the disproportionate smallness of the black female's pelvis and the
larger head of the white child. Caesarean sections are
making child bearing easier now.

Sex, temperature, exercise or work, dope, alcohol,
cigarettes, and clean air all seem to work on one particular
organ, the turbinates in the nose, causing them to shrink or
"the nose to open," allowing the better discharge of the
sinuses, whose openings are controlled by the size of the

turbinates in the nose. In all of these instances, the turbinates are active. Sexual climax and other forms of tranquilization mentioned previously affect the erectile tissue of the turbinates. The erectile tissue in the nasal turbinates is the same type of tissue as in the clitoris and the penis and, like these organs, responds to a substance or hormone that causes a physiological filling of small blood spaces when excited. The penis and clitoris also seem to respond at the same time, activated by the same internal hormone or substance. When a woman reaches a successful climax, these turbinates shrink, like the phallus after climax. This is due to the valves opening and allowing the blood to escape from its entrapment in the vessels, necessary, in the case of the phallus, to maintain a pressure of at least four pounds per square inch to keep it erect. Likewise, small gates in the nasal turbinates and the woman's clitoris are opened up at the same time as if by a single command by the hormone released when the woman climaxes, as well as, and similar to, when the man climaxes. The reduction in engorgement by the blood vessels in the nasal turbinates allows the openings between them from the sinuses to open fully, and sinus discharge flows heavily into the back of the throat and mouth; at the same time, the sinus headaches are relieved, and free air flows into the sinuses, giving the individual a euphoric sensation. If, however, climax is not reached after petting and/or subsequent sex, these turbinates remain engorged, the sinus openings close, active secretions in the sinuses continue; pressure is increased, and this pressure is manifested by severe headaches. Soon the secretions become infected and are released into the blood stream, and the individual develops chills, fever, septicemia (hot flashes), etc. The following day the patient has a headache and is dizzy and nervous. This is the same rebound phenomenon that happens after withdrawal from alcohol, dope, etc. Incidentally, this mechanism may help to explain "hot flashes," for it is simply an occlusion of the sinus openings, a closing up of material within, which gets infected due to mutation of normal bacteria and releases periodically into the blood stream. This causes chills and later "hot flashes" when the heat from muscle fasciculation tries to burn out the invading bacteria in the blood stream. This situation often happens at any age when satisfactory climax is not reached; normal sex at regular intervals always reduces the number of such "hot flashes," when the female can climax regularly.

The modern black man is crowded in the tenseness of the polluted city jungle, where the turbinates swell more due to the pollution. Just as important, the twelve-to-sixteen hour hard, hot labor jobs that he used to have have now been reduced to picking up small objects like pencils, safety pins, etc., thus allowing him to have more energy for "mamma," who is less able to handle his energy. Therefore, he often has to use one of the other modalities previously mentioned for tranquilization.

The white woman, has the wide hips and the wide pelvic outlet needed to deliver babies rapidly, thousands of years ago, in a cold environment. The head of the white baby could not lay on the pelvis long after complete dilatation and effacement by it of the cervix because of the cold climate and the chance of death by pneumonia, etc. This fact actually set the stage for the ultimate physique of the white male and female. They are "boxlike" in configuration, a consequence of necessary environment adaptation through generations of mutations and selected "adaptive" mating. This "boxlike" body today helps determine the destiny of many whites in sports, etc., to aid them in their livelihood as proportionately as the black's body build helps him.

As the white woman's physique affects and dominates the white man's and white woman's physique because of the need for rapid baby delivery thousands of years ago, the black man's body build probably determines that of the black male and female alike. For it is their relatively narrow shoulders and tapered hip configuration that would allow rapid forward mobility in a climate and habitat literally dominated with man-eating animals. Only the swift would survive to live another day and to propagate and perpetuate its kind. The large glutei and hamstrings prosteriorly give credence to the musculature necessary for fast forward starts. It has been said the Achilles tendon of the blacks is more developed than the whites, perhaps for the same reason. This type of body build was apparently necessary for the black man thousands of years ago, and, of course, it probably played a dominant role in the female physique, which may not be the best for child birth. A number of physical adaptations may have ensued from the narrow pelvis. One adaptation could be a large muscular uterine body necessary to push the fetus' head through the narrow pelvic outlet; but, alas, being so large and so muscular, it subjects the black woman to two of the most serious maladies for the black man. The muscles of the uterus lead to more chance for trauma by the relatively long black phallus, particularly when sex is practiced in the missionary way, and more chance for subsequent inflammation and degeneration into fibroids. Both the large size of the fundus and body of the uterus, as well as the fibroids, lead to more pressure on the thin "cordlike" round ligaments to hold the uterus forward, and it therefore falls back into the hollow of the pelvis making it difficult for it to empty. Infection due to increased mutation and increased virulence of prior normal, and now pathogenic, organisms sets in. A vicious circle ensues and spells doom for many black man, black woman relationships.

To compensate for the more narrow muscular pelvic outlet, the black female's uterine musculature became excessive to aid in delivery. This enlarged hypertrophied musculature has worked against the black man in modern society, particularly when he has adapted the white man's ornaments, refinements, and, indeed, even his posture in propagating the species--sexual intercourse the "missionary way." The female on top of the male or the male from the rear are probably more natural positions for the black man. These positions that have probably encouraged the relatively longer length of the black phallus and the smaller, more muscular vagina of the black female, the latter necessary to hold the head of the phallus in the vagina, the longer phallic length, of course, to breach the increased space in the foregoing positions, which I feel were more comfortable in our original hot climate.

We can easily see how the black female's uterus would be encouraged to stay in place with the above position, i.e., anteflexed, and how, with our new adopted position, the "missionary way," the longer phallus, gravity, the shorter vagina, the larger fundus on the top of the uterus, all act to push the uterus into a retroflexed position and initiate a series of "disasters" for the black couple in this "white man's world." The woman-on-top position would allow the black man to keep the relatively large fundus of the black female's uterus pushed forward in a position to drain infection and stagnation of uterine secretions more easily. In an African setting, this would be a much "cooler" approach to sex.

We can see how the environment--the coldness in the north and the "wild" animals near the equator--may have played important roles in the determination of the body build and even the destiny of modern man.

In Africa, the man-on-the-bottom or from-the-rear sexual position probably was practiced before the missionaries arrived, missionaries who had probably practiced sex with the male on top, which, of course, was more desirable in a cold climate where individuals were also in a relatively naked situation. Like the color of the skin and the texture of the hair, nature has allowed certain physical attributes to survive as an adaptation to better propagate the species relative to the environment, which, at that time, was the strongest force controlling man's survival.

In the foregoing pre-missionary position, the black phallus acts to keep the fundus anteflexed and empty of menstrum; and discharge is very easy in that position; whereas in the missionary position, the black male is actually compounding a bad situation and helps develop retroflexion and thus stagnation of the foregoing discharge and chronic infections in the black female.

Other environmental factors may have played a role in

the development of the respective body physiques of the races. To appreciate this fully, we should reflect on our ancestors, who were not clothed or were sparsely clothed, if we are to keep in perspective the full meaning of development of the female. I believe that in the development of the black female, the thighs are proportionately larger than the calves, in contrast to the white female, and the hips are somewhat stream-lined perhaps more than any other group of females.

One of the main objectives that has to be considered when a woman is functionally spayed, because of pelvic disease, is the ability to reach a climax. A climax is necessary for ovarian function, and a potentially functioning healthy ovary is necessary for a climax. When the woman does not climax, she becomes "evil" and nervous like a spayed cat. This may account for a bit of the frustration at this time between the man and woman, which ultimately leads to dissolution of their marriage or relationship. Whether she has been literally spayed because of the disease, or whether she has been under the surgeon's knife and had bilateral oophorectomy, the re-sults are the same.

Therefore, it behooves the male to watch the female's attitude; if she gets irritable or "Sapphirish," like a spayed cat, when a "Tom" is seen, the husband should urge her to have a competent pelvic examination by her physician, specifically, a physician well-trained for black female pelvic problems. If the male is impotent, he should receive treat-ment to correct his problem so that he can excite her ovaries again by adequate sex on a regular basis, thereby reducing the possibility of "hot flashes" and dissolution of the re-lationship. The ultimate climax can best be reached by a potent male phallus, and a healthy female pelvis.

Until recently, the leaving of diseased tubes after a hysterectomy presented problems of abscess formation from the remaining tubes. The tubes should be left in, in order to enhance the supply of blood to the ovaries, which would form cysts if these tubes were removed. These are problems for the operating surgeon that can occur and may possibly subject him to a malpractice suit. Of course, cancer in the remaining ovary remains a very remote possibility. One of the particular problems for the black woman who has a large fibroid uterus, retroflexed and diseased for a long time, is that it obstructs the large vessels in the back of the pelvis and produces an obstructive phenomenon on the pelvic plexus of vessels, thereby increasing the incident of deep phlebitis and pulmonary emboli because of the low pressure head of return of blood to the heart from the legs and pelvis through the obstructed vessels. The black woman who has had many fibroids, etc., becomes prone to embolic disease. The dilemma comes when the phlebitic individual has been spayed; hormones are given her to prevent hot flashes, but they, too, enhance the formation of blood clots and probably cause an increase in morbidity and mortality. I also should mention sickle cell disease trait, which is apparently a Mendelian dominant trait, because I am seeing more and more of it in the black female. This disease trait causes an increase in the formation of blood clots by also increasing the viscosity of the blood.

Other sequelae of disease predominant in the female with large fibroids and coexisting infection are the occurrences of hypertension—for two reasons.

One is the actual obstruction, complete and partial, of the ureters with subsequent back pressure on the kidneys, which causes a kidney mechanism to function and raise the blood pressure from the abnormal stimulus. The second is the occurrence of uretheral stenoses due to recurrent infection and fibroses with contraction of the opening, leading the kidney to produce hypertension by the same mechanism, affection of the Juxto-Glomerular apparatus.

I remember one patient in this instance whose hypertension became "malignant" and who subsequently died of the hypertension disease even though the tumorous uterus had been removed several years previously.

One of the more subtle dilemmas in individuals who do not have their ovaries, in my opinion (and this is not confirmed by investigation), is that the ovaries give a minute-to-minute amount of female hormones, according to the body's demands, and this seems to have some anti-inflammatory potency against "colds" or sinusitis, particularly if the woman gets stimulated at regular intervals by sexual climaxes. If a man can now have sexual relations with her, and she can now reach a climax, with the disease gone, it seems to have a tendency to reduce the swelling of the turbinates in the nose. The turbinates close the opening of the sinuses by their enlargement and may cause pus to form in the sinuses when closed for a long time. When climax is achieved, the valves in the clitoris and the penis and turbinates are all relieved by perhaps the same hormone. The enlargement of the turbinates is reduced, the small openings in the nose between the turbinates that drain the sinuses are therefore opened allowing them to drain, and the female literally has "her nose opened."

When a woman becomes excited and does not reach a climax, several things happen in her sinuses that have had their openings closed by the enlarged turbinates. She gets a severe headache or "bursting" feeling in the prefrontal or sinus area due to the continued secretion of fluid from the walls of the sinuses whose natural drainage opening is blocked. This fluid becomes stagnant like any body fluid that is not allowed to drain; therefore, her sinuses become filled with pus or infection, with subsequent tension building due to putrefaction, gases, etc. The body, in an attempt to burn the infection out, some of which is now in the blood stream, produces heat by causing muscle masses to fasciculate. The female becomes hot, (the "hot flashes"), the muscles become exhausted, showers of bacteria continue into her blood stream, probably from now-infected sinuses, and she becomes "chilled."

A similar, but not as severe, situation occurs in the male. However, he can relieve his frustration when very young by masturbation and exercise, or, as he gets older, by hard work, exercise, alcohol, drugs, etc. The marked increase in use of alcohol by men may, in some way, be related to the increased number of "spayed women," both actually and relatively, that we are producing in our society by tampons, infected abortions, some of the contraceptives, and yes, by promiscuity. All produce disease, literally, and actually ablate ovarian function.

One interesting aspect of the male climax is my belief that there are degrees of male climax that run the gamut all the way from night dreams to masturbation to sex with a young or not so young "hot" woman who, when she climaxes, elicits a maximal response from the male, with complete cleansing of his organs into the female. This situation was probably seen in years gone by when older monarchs culled young girls out of the tribe for this reason--to have their prostate glands cleansed of accumulated infection--so that they could start producing sex hormones in greater amounts again and "revitalize their youth."

The female who has "literally been spayed" early by her female disease will quite often have a considerable build-up of arthritic spicules in the sacroiliac joints and the subsequent spasms and pain in the legs. This has an affect on early formation of deep phlebitis in the calves and thighs but, more than anything else, causes the early calcification in the sacroiliac joints. It is this early calcification that causes the "charley horses" to appear when the lady's legs are widely opened or forced outward during the frenzied moments when she tries to reach a climax. The calcific spicules push into the adjacent nerves coming out of the openings in the sacroiliac joints, causing spasm in the muscles of the legs ennervated by them. Of course, the younger the female, the fewer calcific degenerative changes she has. The more often she has sex, the sooner the charley horses in her legs are reduced, and the sooner she will be able to relax and not be detracted by the impending spasms that her mind has been conditioned to expect as the male becomes rougher, preparatory to his climax, and, of course, simultaneously hers.

As aging sets in, the ovaries are stimulated less often, changes in the vaginal mucosa (due to lack of sex and hormone stimulation), sacroiliac joints, etc., make it increasingly harder for the female to climax; the ovaries become more atrophic and less able to respond, or rebound, after prolonged intervals between climax. It is a vicious circle. There is no doubt in my mind that there is a place for the ovaries and their frequent stimulation as far as delaying old age.

I am firmly convinced that when the public becomes aware of the foregoing facts, and if it is found to be efficacious, that considerable gain can be achieved by transplanting ovaries. I think more economic and social good could result if ovaries were transplanted, particularly in women who have already been spayed or in women who may have cancer or cysts in the ovaries and who might need a transplant at the time of surgery. If compatible ovaries could be found by tissue type, etc., it would be a simple operation to transplant a small sliver of ovary into the rectus muscle in the female's abdomen, approximately a five-to-ten minute task. I think it would save not only a considerable amount of frustration in the female but also in the male, and we should not forget that it is not only the female and the male who are involved in this situation but quite often the whole socio-economic family, including the children. Even if these transplants could not take place, or if they were not effective, I think the knowledge of ovarian effect on the whole family and possible further investigation would be a tremendous asset to the man and spayed woman, who quite often are subjected to anxieties or nervousness, particularly toward each other. Sex becomes particularly frustrating for the female and subsequently involves the male, thus becoming a punishing thing for the woman and the man, and consequently, the children.

If a man is knowledgeable about what is really happening with his wife, I think he would be more considerate of the changes that she is undergoing and, of course, make adjustments to the tremendous tension and energy frustration built up in the wife. Understanding would lead to less rebuttal, more empathy by the black male, and perhaps less direct confrontation and trauma, shooting and killing, cutting, etc. Certainly, it may even lead him to fewer attempts to do the antisocial things that are really killing him, particularly alcohol abuse. It may even allow him to channel his excessive energy, not necessarily into the belly of some young woman, but into more exercise and more constructive things, since the sex outlet, the accepted sex outlet, has been cut off.

The cause of many of these problems has been the stuffing of the vagina with material that will soak up menstrum, and of course, tamponade her cervical opening, thus preventing her menstrual discharge. This basically keeps the old dead tissue and pus in her internal genitalia, causing all types of infection by mutation of her own organisms into very virulent bacteria, particularly the enterococci and E. coli, which are normal inhabitants of the colon and the anus, which is only one-half inch from the vagina.

Intrauterine devices and birth control pills, which act to enhance inflammation, do not seem to be a big help in preventing this chronic pelvic inflammatory disease. IUD's and pills seem to cause much disease or enhance its continuation. If the woman can use a condom or a diaphragm, not only does she have a certain reduction of risk of pregnancy, but she also helps to protect the male's prostate, particularly from the "Ping-Ponging" of germs back and forth into her organs from his organs, and vice versa. By protecting the male's prostate, there may be a reduction in prostatitis and cervicitis and, subsequently, cancer of the prostate, in the long run, as well as cervical cancer. We are simply talking about an everyday disease brought on by the incubation and mutation of the woman's and man's own bacteria into more virulent forms of organisms, simulating the process in true "venereal disease."

In black women, we are dealing with a group of women who have an unusually large amount of fibroids, congenital cysts, etc., which cause retroflexion of the uterus and subsequent infection. There is also a tremendous number of our young women who, while still virgins, have ruptured appendixes and, almost invariably, retroflexion of the uterus and problems throughout their childbearing years.

Black women quite often are treated as though they have been promiscuous and that they have the garden variety of venereal disease. This situation also produces frustration for the black woman and often psychologically prevents her from seeking medical help when needed. The disease continues, with its tremendous social implications and ramifications. We are dealing with physicians and patients who have been programmed to be white--an impossibility--for the white medical rules have to be followed by all men, blacks as well. They are perhaps, of all races, least capable of following them. They are more different from whites than any other race on the face of the earth.

We must realize that most of these situations have nothing to do with venereal disease--syphillis and gonorrhea. They are due to the female's own bacteria changing virulence due to mutation which occurs because of the abnormal length of time the bacteria stay in her, a result of the abnormal position of her uterus which prevents regular and normal discharge of her secretions.

In the female, one of the facts that has emerged recently is that pelvic inflammation and fibroids lead to the formation of deep phlebitis of the legs because of the obstruction of the return of the blood to the heart. The "head" pressure of the venous return to the heart, or the speed that it travels, is reduced considerably, thus allowing for the stagnation of

blood in the lower extremities. This leads to congealing of
the formed elements and clots in the legs and the pelvis.
The reduction in the head of pressure and the increased formation and congregation of the formed elements of the blood
bears a direct relationship to the inflammation that occurs,
as well as marked retroflexion of the uterus and its physical
obstruction. This uterine obstruction can act directly to
obstruct the veins in the back of the pelvis going to the
heart. This leads to pulmonary embolus. This may account
for the probable increase in embolic disease, particularly
when female sex hormones are taken, because the female sex
hormones seem to stir up latent fibroids as well as pelvic
inflammation. There is also a retention of fluid in all tissues. This is seen during hormone taking.

The female, even though she may have two or three babies,
may wind up with fibroids and pelvic inflammation, and find out
that she can no longer reach a climax. She may have a tendency to search around perhaps for a man with a shorter phallus who will not hurt her and maybe she can also achieve
climaxes, for she can tolerate the total length of the shorter
phallus without the excessive trauma by an extremely agres-
sive, elongated phallus, sometimes pushing her diseased internal organs up to half a foot into her "belly."

Another interesting facet of the female genital system is
the development of female homosexuality. We cannot begin to
know the many reasons for homosexuality. I think that much
homosexuality is due to early play by females with each other,
maybe even between sisters. They feel the intimacy of each
other, the warmth of each other's body; a certain amount of
minimal climaxes are received. Of course, this initially may
be received without the social stigma and the competition of
having a male who not only can impregnate the female, but who
can devastate the female's moral character in the community.
Whether these homosexual acts increase, or whether we are
dealing with a hereditary situation, is impossible to say.
I am sure they play a predominant role. I cannot help but
feel that there are some women who have sex relations with a
male and perhaps later may react against the male primarily
because they may have some pelvic inflammatory disease or
pelvic problem, such as retroflexion of the uterus, which
prevents them from reaching a climax.

In subsequent sex acts, these females, who perhaps have
an introduction into male-female sexual intercourse without
the benefit of ever reaching a climax, are prevented from
feeling comfortable or at ease with the straight male, for
they become extremely frigid after repeated frustrating encounters with the male when no climax is reached.

These females, in their prying and searching, perhaps
at a local bridge game, may get into a conversation with

39

another female who has the same problem, and wind up in bed
finding theirs is a much more attractive sexual arrangement
because they can reach a minimal climax. They can have the
subliminal climaxes without the pain and the subsequent
frustration that the elongated phallus will make on the pelvic
abscesses, yet not have the two and three days of "gas" and
pain and nervousness afterward. Unless there is some dramatic
change in the removal of infection, it is very difficult for
a woman to take a chance and allow herself to go back to the
male type of sexual trauma after she has had a homosexual
or other abnormal sexual relationship. Even if she does,
she has to give it much thought for her mind is probably conditioned to the previous trauma that she suffered from the
male phallus when her female organs were abnormal, for her
mind also has to be reconditioned to relax even after the
disease is cured.

    This trauma causes divorces among blacks, because the
black woman with female problems, after so many weeks and months
of trying to accommodate her husband, becomes frustrated. The
sequence of events follows like this: he will come in and
have sex with her; she hurts, and she is still aroused after
the man finishes. Of course, she could not climax and cannot
sleep until perhaps three or four o'clock in the morning,
when, as she cools off slowly, she may get an hour's sleep.
She has to get up and go to her job; she wonders why the foreman nags her. Often, you can tell a woman has problems because she comes into the office with aggressive feelings for
the foreman: he is always after her, or she wants her job
changed. Every night when she comes home, the husband is
there, begging or pulling on her, and then, after petting for
several hours, she makes the statement, "Damn it, I'm not going
to get any sleep, anyway, so I might as well go ahead and have
sex with you," only to wind up with the same frustrating situation that she has had on previous nights. This continues
week in and week out, to the point that the female's nervous
system is completely exhausted. Then she runs into the doctor's office and gets nerve pills which are only a temporary
panacea for her. Finally, she will end up with certain subconscious aggressions toward the male penis, and they are
directed not only toward the male penis that is causing her
this frustration, but also toward the total male. Two people
perfectly in love begin to argue and curse each other over
incidental things. Sometimes they recognize how stupid it is,
but they really do not know what the real problem is, what
is really destroying their marriage, until it is too late.
Sometimes the female will see her doctor. She is given some
cream and ointment, and she receives temporary relief from her
infection, but often the pathology remains, and after three
or four sexual acts by the male, she is "down in her belly"

again. Now the economics of the situation come into play.
The frustrated man cannot afford to continue to pay for this
type of sex. Usually he will have to get some other form of
tranquilizer, either "running" the streets, drugs, alcohol,
gambling, or what have you, in order to exhaust his tremendous energy.

On the other hand, the man might trespass on somebody
else's territory, another man's woman, which might lead to
more shootings and killings--prevalent in the black community.
I think that sexual frustration plays a great role in the
unusually high trauma that blacks inflict on each other. But
more frightening than any of this is the subsequent divorce,
or the friction and cursing before the divorce, particularly
where young children are involved. Soon the black man or
black woman is running downtown, the little money they have
accumulated is completely dissipated on legal fees, etc., and
the children are usually left with the female to be raised.
Another black generation lost; lost because there is no way
that the male child will be able to do anything without the
father image and guidance. The rejected, divorced mother is
usually constantly bombarding the male child about the "no
good so-and-so" former husband who "doesn't make his alimony
payments on time," who is constantly fornicating with this new
woman, who, in the eyes and tongue of the rejected wife, is
always a whore. All of this tirade falls on the impressionable
ears of the fatherless male child, who becomes more frustrated.
It is a wonder that the black male descendant of divorced
parents accomplishes as much as he does; his situation is
often hopelessly frustrating. For the one that he resembles
most is despised by the one he loves most.

The father can be an alcoholic or what have you, but the
fact that he is around in a "compatible" male-female relationship, whether there is divorce or not, acts as a tremendous
guide to the development of the male child, for there are few
situations in which a male child can accomplish anything without fatherly guidance. In our recent societal changes from
rural to city dweller, we have lost the guidance of the
matriarchal grandfather, who was probably the stabilizing force
in the paternalistic rural communities when the husband or
real father was absent.

BLACK WOMAN, WHITE WOMAN;
BLACK MAN, WHITE MAN

This work is dedicated to the black male who lies beside his female companion and hears the familiar chant "I'm tired." "I just don't feel like it." "That's all you want to do." "You don't care if I live or die . . . just so you get your satisfaction." "All you want is my body." "You don't love me."

Likewise, it's dedicated to the female who has to lie beside her companion and hear the familiar "If I ain't getting it, someone else is. What do you do all day? I have to go to work all day, and all you do is lay around the house; you talkin' 'bout you're tired."

In both instances, I think we have situations that are potentially explosive as far as the black male and female are concerned. Potentially explosive because it is a condition that is seen often in black male and female relationships in America, in that our sexual problems are basically behind some of our socioeconomic, mental, and physical confrontations, particularly in America. Of course, there are a lot of other problems that feed this potentially explosive situation. Most doctors, in fact, I would say almost all doctors, in the Western world have been trained to deal with Western people-- white Caucasians -- because it is the white Caucasian's mores that determine the laws, and they write the medical books in order to perpetuate and to best serve that system with which they are familiar.

It is not the purpose of this book to necessarily pick one system or another or to say that it is good or bad. Perhaps, I think that for the most part Western civilization is good; certainly the fact that Western civilization, the white man's entree into Africa, and other situations by which the nuns, missionaries, etc., took along Western mores, etc., have helped the blacks up to a certain point. I do feel that there are certain peculiar physical differences between the white woman and the black woman and between the black man and the

43

white man that allow for certain deficiencies in the system for the black couple, that is, that the system is good, definitely for all people. There are, however, certain specifics that have to be taken into consideration when dealing in a black situation in a white man's culture.

This book is being written primarily to reflect my own personal thoughts or ideas about a particular situation and in no way poses the definite, unwavering truth. That is, it reflects my ideas on different things, and they may not be true, in fact, or may not be true in the minds of other people. In all instances, however, the facts that I have presented are true to my own thinking and beliefs.

Is it true what they say about black men desiring white women? I think so, particularly and almost equally true, as white men desiring black women.

There are several reasons for this. I think the primary reason is the ability of the white man to keep the white woman at arm's length from the black male and I think that throughout history one finds that the dominant group, in order to remain dominant, has to sustain a certain amount of "mystique" about his women as "untouchables." This is one reason that there is an unusual attraction of black men to white women. By doing this, the white man can't practice the old minister's axiom of "do as I say, not as I do," and therefore has to literally keep hands off black women, particularly in the light of day.

Another factor at work is the ability of the white woman to convey a certain white cultural advantage that she has enjoyed over the past, while the black woman was in slavery and in Africa. The black woman was relatively Western culturally disadvantaged during this time and not quite as competitive as the white woman, that is, in the "white culture" in which we live.

Still another advantage that the white woman has that seems attractive to the black man is the relative abundance of available educated black women compared to educated black men. Due to several factors, one of them being that the Southern black woman is not only encouraged to go to school, but is often subsidized by the dominant white male group in the South to the disadvantage of the black male, in fact, to his definite deprivation of education and cultural outlets. So what you have is a disproportionate number of educated black women to black men. This means that the culturally advanced black woman is more in abundance and therefore less attractive to the black male because of the basic law of supply and demand; the more supply, the less demand for a commodity.

Along the same reasoning, there may be a genetic or hereditary larger proportion of black females, particularly

of the marriageable age, than there are black males; a ratio
of ten to seven has been mentioned: ten black females to
seven black males.

There are certain African countries that have a ratio
sometimes as great as two to one of black females to males,
and, of course, this may be one cause of polygamy in certain
African countries. For the black female's basic genital problems have brought about an adaptation in the race to increase
the number of females for survival. This could be for several
reasons. In Africa, where there are many tribal wars, you
find that the death rate of the black male is excessively
higher than the females. Also, the male baby is not as strong
as the female baby in all races and therefore has a higher
mortality rate. Fibroids and subsequent pelvic complications,
of course, are always an overriding factor in higher black female morbidity and early mortality, expecially during childbirth. Thus more females are necessary to maintain the basic
survival ratio of ten to seven for blacks.

The white female has a very small uterus and shallow
pelvis and therefore does not have the associated retroflexion,
fibroids and pelvic inflammations that the black female has,
which makes the possibility of sexual play with the white woman more frequent in a male-female relationship. In other
words, the white female is perhaps more durable sexually than
the black female and therefore has less "down time" than her
sexually fragile black counterpart with the small, often
contracted anthropoid pelvis. It is the foregoing pelvic
inflammation that makes it painful for the black woman to
reach a climax, which therefore makes her more frigid. I feel
that the white woman often has, without associated retroflexion
and disease, a much better ability to enjoy or at least to
tolerate, the excessive trauma heaped upon the female by the
black male. This also may account in large part for the black-
complexioned man particularly to be strongly attracted to the
lighter-complexioned black female, whose pelvic organs often
closely simulate those of the white woman.

All in all, the white female has developed, over tens of
thousands of years, perhaps through adaptation, into a being
who is ideal for this system. In fact, this system was developed specifically for this individual, therefore making it
a situation like an automatic response. The individual in
that type of situation can do so many things automatically,
without the energy dispensed in using conscious thought.
Whereas blacks, both male and female, because the system was
not designed for either of them, have to spend so much time
and energy actually thinking out every move consciously. They
are at a disadvantage from the beginning, for they are competing
with the white man and white woman, who can do so many things
by reflex or automatic action, leaving them with much more re-

45

serve energy than a black man or woman in the same situation.
The recent Baake case reflects how white I.Q.'s should be
higher, for white's make up the tests. It would be the opposite if blacks made up the tests. Also, it is easy to see
how some black movie stars, men or women who are in a position
to move or desirous to move up, would receive considerable
help from a white mate in this situation, male and/or female.
It would seem that everything that the white partner would
say would automatically be recorded as the gospel because they
could be so accurate in their interpretation or predictions of
how the system would work that it would awe the black man or
woman to no end.

The white woman also has more tools to work with in this
system. She can insinuate herself into the clubs, into the
power circles that make decisions; she can overhear certain
policies and policy statements simply by being invisible in the
white world. It would make it very easy for her to be a
tremendous asset to a black man "on the rise." She can get
jobs easier and understand the system better than the black
woman, and, of course, she is not subject to recriminations
by other whites for often they do not know the source of their
power. A Jew masquerades as an Episcopalian, a Catholic
masquerades as a Jew, etc.

The white female has been so held back from the black
male that she becomes quite a source of accomplishment, particularly for "programmed" black men. It is very complicated,
but I think that, all in all, if one could give one reason for
the attraction it is that the white woman knows the system
better and can interpret it to the black man better than the
black woman. This may be one of the causes of the disproportionate number of white female-black male marriages. In any
event, it may not only be the color of her skin or the straight-
ness of her hair that attracts the black male.

However, the reduced "down time" sexually of the white
female compared to the black female is undoubtedly the overriding causative factor in many instances of black male-white
female marriages, at least initially.

Keep in mind, however, that the underlying causes for some
black-white marriages occur in the instances in which the black
male feels he is not aggressive or adequate enough to make his
own way in the white man's society; that is, he is programmed
to feel inferior to the white man.

A white male-black female relationship runs into problems
because of the smallness of the anthropoid-type pelvis of the
black female, making it almost imperative that the fetus of
the relationship be delivered by caesarean section, for the
baby, in most instances, will probably have the larger head
of the white fetus; more complications and subsequent "down
time" sexually in this type of relationship -- thus, frustra-

tion, as mentioned previously.

The larger head of the white fetus may also be a consequence of thousands of years of birthing children in a cold
climate where the white woman during delivery was subjected
to the rigors of having to birth a child rapidly after complete dilation and effacement of the cervix. The head of the
fetus acts as a "battering ram" to open up the passageway for
delivery. It is conceivable that a child with a smaller head
would not dilate and efface the cervix adequately enough for
the wide shoulders and the wide pelvis of the whites, and the
small headed child and/or the mother would die in the process,
during the prolonged and hard delivery in a very rough climate -- leaving the larger headed fetus and mother to perpetuate the race. Of course, it may be a case of what came
first, the larger head or the wider pelvis.

It is said that the rich white planters in the South
during slavery would have the poor "hillbilly" women from the
mountains come to the plantation to mate with the black males
in order to breed lucrative mulattos and quadroons to ship to
New Orleans, then to Europe as house servants. The pure black
African female could not serve the purpose if she mated with
white men because of her narrow pelvic outlet and increased
possibility of death during labor and normal delivery of the
larger-headed "white baby" because caesarean sections were not
feasible then. The foregoing may help to account for less
frequent attachment between white men and black women than
there seems to be between black men and white women, particularly for "lasting relationships."

The black man, I think, is quite overactive sexually.
It is this energy that the black male has, to an excessive
degree, that he has not had to expend in his work recently,
as in the previous generations when he had to work the fields
from sun up until he could not see; often, the full moon would
then come out. Now his major outlet is in sexual play or
alcoholism, either of which will exhaust this tremendous
energy, for his muscles are now unflexed because of the machines
of industry.

I do not feel that the white male is as sexually aggressive as the black man. He doesn't seem to have or at least
doesn't exhibit the aggressive physical energy that the black
male seems to have to exhaust. And, of course, having a
shorter, wider phallus in the relatively small, proportionately,
vaginal outlet of the black female reduces the number of contacts and flipping of the uterus into the retroflexed position
sexually and, I think, makes these two individuals more compatible sexually if they do not have children. Indeed, it may
have been a cause for the missionary position to have developed
in blacks, for the male white missionaries with shorter,
proportionately, larger phalluses may have had some difficulty

in sex with young or virginal black females which was probably
their prerogative under the circumstances and, therefore, had
to continue the male-on-top position for entrance into the
vagina.

He probably had to assume this position in order to maintain himself in the introitus, particularly since this was his
basic comfortable position of sex in a cold climate. Therefore, he set this "missionary position" down as law and proper.
This has been the bane of the black man's existence during the
last several hundred years.

Even with this being the case, the missionaries probably
had some difficulty entering these black females, if it is true
that the white male's phallus is shorter but larger in diameter
than the black male's phallus.

In perpetuating the system of sex in this fashion, he
may have converted the black female's mind into cohabiting
the white way and corrupted the black male/female's sexual
position perhaps for centuries.

This attempt to copy methods and programs that the white
man has laid down, even though he may have done it honestly,
because that is something that is natural for him, has, I
think, quite often led to considerable confusion in the black
community.

With the black phallus being longer in length, a different
position in sex would have a tendency to keep the uterus anteflexed and therefore empty of secretions, particularly the
menstrual secretions. It is these menstrual secretions, more
than anything else, that cause the incubation of the patient's
own bacteria, particularly from the anus and oral cavity and
the subsequent inflammation and frigidity that occur. This
usually occurs early in the marriage, particularly if there
is a hampering of egress of discharge from the uterus, for
example cervical stenoses, retroflexion of the uterus, obstruction by fibroids, or wearing of tamponading structures
during menstruation.

The female-on-top position or sex from the rear may have
been practiced by blacks due to Africa's excessive heat, thus
giving a rationale for the relatively long black phallus.

The black mind may also be conditioned by things that
happen in the white community because the white woman, whose
uterus is usually smaller, has little problem with retroflexion of the uterus. Therefore, the only time that she
would be bothered with female problems would be due to venereal
origin, or gonorrhea or herpes, probably with the same inci-
dence as the black female, relatively. And because of this,
physicians who treat black as well as white women, are programmed into thinking that this is what happens any time that
the woman has a discharge.

My contention is that there is a whole world of difference

between the black pelvis and the white pelvis. It is true
that the black female has gonorrhea or venereal disease
relatively as often as the white woman. But I feel that there
is a tenfold increase of pelvic inflammation in the black
pelvis over the white pelvis, which is not due to venereal
disease. But most black and white physicians trained with
white standards often have an attitude toward these individuals and sometimes verbalize this attitude, with the end
result that often the black woman will wait until the last
moment or until the disease becomes chronic before she seeks
help, for she is so afraid of being embarrassed by the situation, although, in most instances, it was innocently arrived
at.

The difference is, perhaps as much as anything, in the
attitude that they assume during intercourse. Couple this
with the fact that the black man is forced to adapt the missionary attitude toward his female, which is unnatural for
him, this makes it very difficult for the black male to ad-
vance out of the sex act, socioeconomically. The primary
reason for this is due to the fact that a tremendous amount
of his income and time is tied up in the sexual aspect of his
living because of the disease in his female partner and an
equal amount of ignorance by the medical society in handling
it because of their white programming. This makes it more
difficult for him to assert himself into economic and other
areas of endeavor, for he exhausts much of his income ob-
taining sexual gratification.

In addition to the missionary way mentioned above, which
leads to infection and retroflexion of the uterus, are the
following problems for the black female: the inherently
larger fundus, or top of the uterus, and the fact that she may
have longer tubes. The fact that her pelvis is deeper, being
wider from front to back, allows more room for the uterus and
tubes to be retroflexed and subsequently to be fixed in this
position. Her smaller and much more muscular vaginal introitus than her white counterpart allows her to excessively massage the male phallus and perhaps excite him to a higher form
of eroticism, or higher form of ejaculation. Under these
circumstances, the muscle around the prostate gland, where
quite often several abscesses are formed in the older male,
has a tendency to contract harder and perhaps in contraction
burst the abscesses out of the fibrous cocoon in which the
body has confined them. These abscesses are the results of
infections that are quite often a consequence of previous
sexual contacts. These infections are emptied into the belly
of the black female, particularly the young black females.

Once this infection gets a "hold" on the female, particularly if her uterus is retroflexed, it remains there as a
chronic infected condition, that I feel may be involved in the

49

formation of fibrous tumors, along with trauma of intercourse, particularly when the phallus pounds the body of the uterus backward and when coitus is practiced exclusively in the missionary position by blacks.

One of the other aspects or thoughts on this matter is the idea of why blacks were slaves. I think that blacks and whites are exact opposites or more different in features, idealogy, etc., than all other races. That is, that the white man and woman are exact opposites of the black man and woman, as far as human beings are concerned, this made it easier for the white man's conscience to have adapted the black man as a slave rather than other ethnic groups. The rationale of this is the more dissimilarity you see in a group of people, the better your chances are of adjusting your mind to this great evil that you are doing, for example, slavery. This concept may help account for the difficulty that blacks have in advancing in this country today. For there is no race of people I know of who are not given a better break than the American black man in society. Some of it may be due to the easy identity or high visibility of blacks and the ability to keep them out of the power cliques because of this identity. But much of it is due to the white man's ability to identify all other races with some of his physical characteristics, hair, keen nose, etc., more than he can with the black man, even though blacks are probably the second oldest major American group. It is possibly related to the biblical passage that reads: "God made man in the image of himself." Therefore, the white man can more easily rationalize his hatred and fears toward the black man than he can with any other racial group for example that has identifying characteristics similar to his straight hair or keen features.

There are other factors that enter into it because as things become more like you, the more beautiful they are to you. Over the years, we adjust things in beauty according to how close they approach our particular standards. For this reason it was easier for the white man to adjust to the black man in slavery because of this tremendous difference, more so than with the Asian, the southern Europeans, or the Indians.

Of course, the other thing is that when the white man did have these types of individuals as slaves, such as the Indian slaves or indentured servants in America, it only took a generation or two before these people became assimilated because of their similarities, and the marriage of a beautiful young slave lass to the son of the master took place.

I think blacks have genealogically inherent desires to trust people, as opposed to whites, whom I feel are more conniving and deceitful in their particular genealogy. One of the reasons that this has occurred is because of the part that the environment has played in the modification of the skins, etc., of individuals. The same basic role was developed in the individual's psychological ability to trust or not to trust, as in his physical differences, made possibly by adaptations necessary for survival.

By that I mean that the blacks had been raised in an African situation where they were prone to have almost everything handed down to them on a silver platter. They had no reason to connive or be deceitful for food or other things, whereas the white man had to grub for just about everything they ever received in Europe, e.g., to the point where deceit and conniving sometimes meant the difference between whether they would eat or starve to death during the long, cold, barren winters.

This is in no way meant to be a reflection on the intelligence or intellect of either group, because I feel that blacks had things, nondeceitful things, that gave them more time to do a lot of reflective thinking, and keep their minds sharply developed, for the male had to hunt every day in order to survive. The white man survived by virtue of his ability to connive and plan, and I think it is this latter genealogical attribute by which the white man today excels in material areas. I feel that the emphasis on racial differences should be on adaptation for survival rather than any evolutionary theories, for modern man started out together, black and white, perhaps millions of years ago, and mentally they are still equal. The black man can possibly think faster than the white man. The white man can program better.

There is also difficulty for the black man to make sexual adjustment either through medical care for his wife, or perhaps even through pills and tranquilization to reduce his excess energy and be competitive with the white man, who makes the rules and changes them at the "drop of a hat" to best fit his needs. Blacks should be allowed to get into situations where their excessive energy can be channeled to their own good, rather than to the good of the white man. Interestingly enough, it may be in this area where the white man in the United States has been able to surpass other countries by using the excessive energy of the black man that has been poured into the industries and the farms of this country, allowing the white man time to reflect and to develop certain engineering and scientific feats, as well as the artistic feats that have put him ahead of the rest of the world.

We have to also consider one characteristic of differences between black and white, and that is that one has to recognize that the total internal environment, black people/white people, is almost the same. It is only the external environment, genital organs, skin, nose, color, etc., that I feel separate us, and these differences were primarily brought on by external surroundings and environment. Even the internal differences

51

are environmentally produced. The ability of the black man to sweat and thus dissipate heat, coupled with his black skin and kinky hair to reflect the sun's rays made him ideal for the raising of cotton and sugar cane -- a much better choice than the white indentured servants that the slave owners could have gotten much cheaper.

In fact, this ability to sweat and dissipate heat probably was the basic reason that blacks entered the factories in the North during the last four decades for they were invariably placed in the foundry and "hot" areas where it was difficult for whites to work because of their inability to throw off heat as well as the blacks.

The black child, by being subjected to this dominant white culture, is brainwashed into becoming a loss in life in a futile effort at trying to be white. Certainly in an integrated situation in which the young black child during his formative years is subjected to the white society, especially from the age of two to fourteen, he becomes extremely traumatized by the realization that he is being dominated by a society that idolizes none of the physical attributes that he possesses. He therefore becomes a pawn; a child in bondage, mentally, to the total black-white misfit situation. Within his impressionable mind, he becomes ashamed of his heritage and ashamed of the color of his skin and the shape of his nose. What makes these situations so difficult for him to overcome is that they are impressed on him during his formative years, never to be released from his mind as to what actual beauty is or what actual beauty is not. Because of this, he carries this burden of feeling inferior for the rest of his life. Unfortunately, the "light" does not come along after his formative years. I think he could better cope with it if it did. The result is that black people, forty years of age, are still dyeing their hair red and still lightening their skins because it has been impressed indelibly on their minds by the traumatic experiences since before entering primary school as black Americans. If he were older when he became exposed to the white culture, he would be able to tolerate the situation much better because he would become very understanding and possibly could develop his own ideas about life, and "whiteness" would not be as impressionable to him-- in some instances--but unfortunately, his basic pattern of life is determined during his formative years.

The black leaders that we have, almost always perpetuate the white rule by, one: being the black who best emulates the white way, two: being the black who acts the way the white system has designed or programmed that he acts, and three: as a leader, acts as an umbrella of gendarmes or black flunkies to assure that any black leadership will continue to be individuals who fall in the above three categories.

Black women who are frigid by virtue of oophorectomy or pelvic inflammation disease, use sex as a lever to gain control of the male and the household, for she has no desire for sex. Sex punishes her, therefore she will often barter herself to gain complete control of the black male. This results in a black matriarchal society in the U.S., whereas in Africa, as I understand, the household is patriarchal which is probably natural also for American blacks. Polygamy did probably help maintain the social situation in Africa.

Although the frigid black female controls the household, it is usually an uneasy truce, or artificial position for her and the male. The male winds up hating the female in the matriarchal system, and often strikes back even violently to this unnatural situation. In any event, there is no living with the woman who has been oophorectomized either actually or relatively. This, of course, may be one of a number of compensatory mechanisms produced by nature to reduce the possibility of pregnancy in the female with infection. Similar natural mechanisms are seen with prematurity, tubal pregnancy, spontaneous abortions, etc., all of which are orchestrating to prevent the delivery of a "bad seed." And the more babies a woman has, the more damage to her organs, the more problems with sex, the more frigidity and automatically fewer babies.

Hopefully, this book will at least give some insight into the problems that blacks are having, because usually the problems that blacks have are between the man and the woman. On the other hand, the problems that whites have, when they have problems, are not between the man and the woman but between the generations, the younger to the older. In that situation, this problem is resolved by the youngsters growing older.

But the problems in the black community are not resolvable usually in a lifetime. And if this information is received as I am trying to give it, it may encourage the black male to have more empathy for the problems that daily frustrate the black female, which of course, in a vicious circle, frustrates his problem for survival, and vice versa.

The Japanese, and to a certain extent the Chinese, prevented the ingress of whites and missionaries into their country during the time that all races were coming out of the "dark ages." For the most part, they maintained their culture, and prevented the tremendous "deculturing job" done to the black man in America and to a certain extent Africa and other areas where "Western culture" touched. The Japanese and Chinese maintained their specific sexual relationships.

Nigeria and other African countries reflect perhaps some of the disruptive aspects of the entrance of Western monogamous culture into a polygamous culture. They have gone from countries who exported food etc., and are now countries who not only import food but in wide areas are starving to death.

PSYCHOLOGICAL AND OTHER FACTORS OF SEX

The female with pelvic disease discovers, night after night, quite often, that she will be subjected to the same procedure by the male. He will "pet" her and "pet" her, and finally she will become angry and say, "Go ahead because I can't sleep, anyway," and she becomes excited again. She goes through the same process again the next night and is always unable to reach a climax because of her disease. Then, by the end of several weeks, the woman is so tired and aggravated that she becomes very "frigid." It is this type of frigidity that I think accounts for the most frigidity that we see in women.

However, there are other psychological factors that may lead to frigidity, although I do not feel that these psychological problems are very important except in isolated individual cases. The lack of orgasm brought on by anxiety from location, that is, a back seat of an auto, a dirty motel room, expecially where vermin may interfere at any time, a nosy mother-in-law, or young children who could inadvertently walk into the "love parlor," or bedroom, at any moment, excessive noise, heat, cold, etc., all of these situations, if repeated often enough, can lead to frigidity.

There is also the preconditioning by a mother who can psychologically insert guilt feelings of sex into a woman that, if not handled properly, can continue throughout the patient's or individual's sex life.

And, of course, there is always the physical attributes of the partner: his looks, his smell, his family tree, his manly desire or nondesire, his money. There is the fear of pregnancy or the fear of social diseases, such as gonorrhea, syphillis, herpes, etc., all of which have one central theme; the inability of the woman to be completely at ease, both physically and psychologically, to be comfortable in the act. If the latter is not achieved, any of the foregoing can lead to no orgasm, and if repeated often enough, to frigidity, either temporary or, in time, permanent.

The black uterus, the body of it and the fundus have to
be large and muscular to push the baby's head out of a small
pelvic outlet. The round ligaments, two cords that hold the
fundus and body of the uterus forward, the large parts of the
uterus, are therefore somewhat more strained to hold them forward in the black woman than in the smaller-sized uterus of
the white woman. If the uterus falls backward into the bottom
of the pelvis, this abnormal position allows for accumulation
of menstrum and tubal infection. We can see how the relative
angle of the thrust of the male phallus can enhance the normal
position of the uterus or hurt it. If it comes in from the
rear or with the female on top, there would be a tendency of
the body and fundus to fall forward with the aid of gravity.
However, if it comes in from the male on top, there would be
a tendency to aggravate the abnormal or tilted uterus at the
moment of climax.

The foregoing relaxed situations are absolutely necessary
for the female to evacuate conscious thoughts from her cerebral
cortex before she can become the "total lower animal," who is
without cerebral cortex, a physiological necessity for complete
climax in the female and the release of all of the important
unknown hormones that cause necessary changes in the body's
systems only with climax. The aggravated woman whose ovaries
cannot be stimulated by climax is like a "spayed cat." One
vital area that is affected by the ovary function is the mucous membrane of the vagina for the integrity of its hardness,
which, during good sex periods, is like the palm of the hand.
This hard-skinned vagina is maintained by functioning, often-
stimulated ovaries, and when this does not happen, the vaginal
mucous membrane reverts to the prepubertal configuration, like
the soft back of the hand, tender and therefore subjected to
tearing microscopically by the penetrating phallus and subsequent invasion into its depths by local bacteria, particularly
around the urethral orifice. This causes cystitis or "New
Bride's Disease," a burning on urination and, at times,
bleeding. Women whose ovaries do not function, whether due
to age (too young or too old), protracted inactivity or having
been spayed, also go through this.

I think that it might help the people who hire a black
woman or any woman, to be allowed to go into not only the
pelvic situation of that particular woman, or the sexual
functionings between her and her partner, because I really do
believe that the amount of productivity by the individual
woman is partly a reflection of her pelvic condition. Also,
it reflects the amount of productivity of her paramour. In
other words, I think that big industrial companies that hire
black or white men and/or women should possibly examine the
female before allowing her or her consort to get into a

position of extreme power because I think that it is the female's pelvic organs that quite often determine the success of the particular employee or his spouse in the establishment. This examination should be handled by individuals who are educated in the realm of the sex organs, the entire body, and its relationship to the sex organs.

This book is perhaps argumentative, but I do not feel the need to defend any of my statements. There are certainly no scientific journals that I can refer to, to substantiate my position. The book strives to cause blacks to reflect, to serve as a guide to a condition that is particular or peculiar to them. In the long run, it may make for better adaptation by the blacks into the Western world as we know it. By a better adaptation or better knowledge of oneself, I think we can compensate for, or modify, a particular situation knowledgeably in order to overcome it. In the total picture, as the black man begins to become knowledgeable of himself and how he relates in a different-ruled world that is foreign to his genealogy and physical make-up, he will, in turn, help the white race because the whole world is totally integrated, and much comfort or discomfort by the least of us means more comfort or discomfort to all of us.

THE NATURE OF ORGASM

The following are quotations from others concerning
orgasms.

"After the accumulating tensions of the preceding contacts have brought me to a state of intense anticipation and excitement, I feel the onset of orgasm at the
precise instant that I perceive the first convulsive
contraction of the phallus in my vagina, simultaneously
the orgastic spasm of my husband's whole body. The
essence of the supreme moment is such that its increase
by further stimuli would be impossible and beyond my
power to endure. Then, I feel liquid warmth of the
ejaculation which gives a perfectly distinct sensation
gloriously soothing and exciting at the same time. It
enables me to receive unimpaired delight and benefit
from the concluding ejaculatory moments. Without over-
strain, these stimuli afforded by the spasm and the soothing libations of the seminal liquid are so complete and
harmonious that my enjoyment remains at a summit, until
my husband's orgasm ceases."

In a more modern sex manual:

"As a woman approaches orgasm, the whole base of her body
accelerates. The heart rate zooms up to 160 or more,
respiration gives way to panting and groaning. In the
meantime, the pelvis is going wild. All the veins in
the pelvic area are at the point of bursting. The vulva
is throbbing rhythmically, to the point of grabbing the
penis. The sensory nerves are at their peak; they are
opened up to each fine drop of sensation. So much current is drawn by the sexual act that the lights in the
cerebrum begin to dim."

The foregoing description represents some of the most
pertinent points about orgasms. Contrary to some writings,
the so-called clitoral orgasm is really a misnomer. There is
only one orgasm, and that is the complete penetration of the

available male phallus into the vagina to the hilt, literally, and the acceptance by the female of this in a situation that is conducive to this height of sexual arousal. I think that in the woman the sexual activity, physiologically, is needed more than in men. Sex and orgasm are the ultimate human act. The particular woman must have a complete and totally concentrated enjoyment of the sexual act. The complete penetration of the available penis into the vagina causes a certain amount of ecstatic "trauma" to the plexus of Frankenhauser and it is this "trauma" that causes the spasmodic contractions and release of material in other areas of the body, such as the sweat glands, oil glands, lungs, sinuses, etc. There is a literal cleansing of the woman when orgasm occurs. The bottom line for this is, of course, reproduction or pregnancy.

Normally, the woman's vagina is approximately 2-3 inches long. This means that there is a movement of the internal organs of the female's genital system up to 5 or 6 inches every time the penis thrusts into her. The phallus, of course, gets larger right at that moment of orgasmic climax. My interpretation of what actually happens in orgasm is that there is a movement out of the cerebrum to the lower brain level of an unknown "center of orgasm," where the movement becomes automatic, similar to the beat of the heart from the cardiac center or to the respirations of the respiratory center. It comes out of control from the damping effect of the cerebrum and its cortex, which is the highest center for man. It becomes an automatic, autonomic type of response. This is an extremely important point of this book.

It is the inability of many black women to allow this movement from the cerebrum to the automatic or autonomic center during attempts at orgasm or reaching climax because of the marked amount of fibroids and infections with which she is plagued. Thus, she has pain at the height of the climax or the fear of pain from conditioned response of previous nights. What enhances this movement to the automatic centers? There must be a complete physical and mental ability of the woman to relax totally. What prevents her from relaxing is, for the woman who has infections, tumors, etc., a conditioned reflex from previous traumatic acts of intercourse, the amount of pain that she receives due to the movement of the phallus pushing the infected female internal genitalia up to one and one-half times the length of her vagina into her abdomen. An individual with tumors or tubal abscesses would have a very hard time relaxing at the precise split second timing necessary to coincide with her husband's orgasm. The pus tubes being pushed against the inside of the pelvis would, perhaps, rupture through the outer lateral opening of the tubes being pushed against the inside of the pelvic wall; perhaps, rupture through the inner aspect as well. This, in turn, causes lo-

calized pelvic peritonitis which causes obstruction of the
intestine through what is known as a paralytic ileus at that
site. This obstruction causes an accumulation of gas, all
the way up to the female's stomach. This causes considerable
discomfort or "gas" to the female which can last for several
days, until the body can clear up the pus from the pelvis,
and normal intestinal peristalsis can move food along its
tract at a specified rate. All of this leads to the conditioning of the black female, somewhat like Pavlov's experiments.

The black female with organic pelvic disease becomes
conditioned, after repeated attacks of sex, to the fact that
as the man's muscles tighten approaching climax, she has to
tighten her thigh muscles to avoid being hurt, because the
male gets rough and plunges hard into the female before
ejaculation. When the female does not tighten herself, the
man has the ability to push his phallus deep into the depth
of the female's vagina and move her internal organs, causing
her pain if she is not healthy, and ecstatic climax if she is
healthy. Over a period of weeks and months, one can see how
the female becomes conditioned to tightening or guarding herself from the thrusting of the hard phallus if she is not
healthy. When the female tightens herself she is then prevented
from the "split-second" relaxation, which is absolutely
necessary for the female reaching a climax, for she is still
cerebrating.

Interestingly enough, during treatment there is a point
when the infected female relaxes with the pus tubes and thus
climaxes. The hard phallus ruptures the abscessed tubes, pus
pours into the peritoneal cavity as well as into the uterus
and vagina. The following day or two a heavy foul discharge
is noticed by the female who then accuses her lover, errone-
ously, of infidelity--more confusion, arguments, and distrust
for the black couple.

When the female does not reach a climax, this also sets
up a vicious circle because she gets all "hot and bothered"
during the act of "petting" or coitus without climax. Her
clitoris becomes engorged, etc., and it takes several hours
of "non-sleep" for her to "cool off." This female may not be
able to get to sleep until later every morning--maybe she gets
one or two hours of sleep per night--and then she has to get
up early and start another day. This is very frustrating and
could, in time, change the female's personality and attitude
toward her spouse, thus leading to marital friction. This
act is repeated over and over again until, over a period of
several weeks or months, the female becomes totally exhausted
nerve-wise, as well as sexual-wise. She then seeks nerve
pills, alcohol, or dope to soothe her nerves--or she resorts
to divorce, a search for a man with a smaller phallus, or, in
some extreme instances, she may seek other females for sexual

companionship, for then she does not have to fight the phallus and can still achieve a certain amount of eroticism.

In the world we are living in today, there is so much stress on the individual that tranquilization is necessary for both male and female. This lack of adequate tranquilization by sex may account for the marked increase in the use of pills and alcohol today. Certainly, I feel that the psychiatrist, psychologist, analyst, have the same meaning in their approach to the basic causes of frigidity in women, but I believe that psychological causes of frigidity are relative. The look and smell of the male, whether or not children are in the next bedroom and may burst in at any moment, the previous conditioning of the female regarding sex psychologically, the size of the male's phallus, the sanction of the act through marriage, etc., all play a role in the climax. However, I feel that they are minor roles to the ultimate situation of the woman with a healthy pelvis. I believe that, in many instances, the healthy woman, if she were not restrained by man's cultural bric-a-brac, would, on a given day, have sexual relations with almost any healthy male. The sexual drive in the healthy female, in most instances, approaches nymphomaniacal proportions because the climax so affects the woman's health and well-being. It causes her sinuses to open (thus, the phrase "he's got your nose open"), whereas, when the act is not terminated in climax for the female, the turbinates remain engorged, shutting off the sinus drainage openings, often causing the patient to have headaches for several hours or even days afterward. This effect on the sinuses, skin, etc., seems to be mediated by a hormone elaborated only after the woman reaches a climax. More on this later.

Women who do not reach a climax usually find that the turbinates in their nose become engorged and enlarged, and the following day they have a terrific headache, dizziness, and "gas." The latter is due to slow draining of the pus into the G.I. tract from the sinuses, plus the paralysis of the gut due to the trauma of the act on inflammed pelvic tissue, particularly "pus tubes." Women, it seems, who have been "spayed" or who have a lot of pelvic infection, cannot reach a climax. They seem to continue in a perpetual state of swollen turbinates and pus formation due to stagnation of secretions in the sinuses. Abscesses in the tubes are pinned between the pelvic bone and the hard phallus during intercourse, particularly at climax, for the male phallus becomes "super hard" and "super long" and ruptures the tubal abscesses into the free peritoneal cavity. This causes paralysis of the bowels or ileus, allowing undigested material in the upper portion of the G.I. tract to stay too long in the pelvis due to paralysis of the gut below. Subsequent putrefaction takes place, causing "gas" and misery for the female for several days after intercourse, until the body can control the pus and reconfine it into the tubes or pyosalpinx.

These situations, particularly as they concern the diseased female pelvis, condition the female's mind for future encounters with the phallus, particularly at the split second before ejaculation when the phallus becomes harder and perhaps longer. Since her mind is conditioned by repeated abuses at that time and the subsequent sequelae as noted above, she "tightens up" to prevent the hard-thrusting phallus from entering her maximally at the moment that she should be relaxing preparatory to the climax, and the magic moment fleetingly passes her by. As a result, more engorgement of the turbinates in the nose, for the "adrenalin-like" material to reduce engorgement was not released, for she did not reach a climax; headaches ensue, and paralysis of the intestines and "gas" build up for several days for the female who has pelvic inflammation. It is like a "vicious circle."

The foregoing, coupled with the relatively longer black phallus, the larger fundus of the black female uterus, the stuffing of the very small muscular black female's vagina with tampons at menstruation so that she can look chic in her tight-fitting slacks--but more than anything else, the "missionary way" of sexual intercourse by blacks, all have combined to throw the uterus into retroflexion to start the chain of infection and fibroids, etc.

The Bartholin glands, chronically infected probably as a consequence of the hard delivery by black females, often serve as a nidus of repeated infection in the black couple.

The big crux of most illnesses today is the run-of-the-mill sinusitis. A lot of it is related to the sex act, especially when the black woman, or the white woman, has intercourse and practices coitus interruptus. The sequence of coitus interruptus is that the man inserts his penis, and just before he reaches his climax, withdraws it hoping that this will keep the woman from becoming impregnated.

This is a mechanical thing that robs the female of the moment of the climax because it is at this time, when the male's penis swells to its largest size, and when it penetrates to the deepest part of the vaginal vault, that the woman is able to reach her climaxes and subclimaxes. This is because, as noted earlier, the thought process in the brain shifts from the cerebral cortex to the lower centers, from the conscious to the subconscious, and then the lady merely lets herself go, totally relaxes, and reaches a climax that is a physiologic necessity in any act. If she doesn't reach this climax, she winds up disturbed, unable to sleep until four or five o'clock in the morning. The next day, she is nervous, tense, and extremely bitchy--and becomes "Sapphirish."

This is not only a physical thing; it can be a mental thing because, in some instances, the woman feels that if she enjoys it, in her mind, or reaches a climax, she will become pregnant. So, in her thought processes, when this good feeling comes, through her conditioned thinking, instead of relaxing and enjoying it, she will tighten up or move out from under the man in order to prevent it. By doing this, in her mind, conception is prevented. This is not too very far from the truth because I believe there is more than a causal relationship between the climax and the extrusion of the ova from the ovary at that moment thereby enhancing impregnation, particularly around the fifteenth day of the menstrual cycle.

This could also be considered a thought pattern in the minds of some women in which they feel it is punishment to have this good feeling; so rather than allow themselves to reach a climax, they will jump out from under the man or deny themselves this enjoyment, a sort of inner punishment for the sin of enjoying sex.

Whether it is coitus interruptus or pelvic disease or whatever that prevents the female from totally relaxing, totally climaxing, the results are the same. The turbinates are enlarged, the sinuses are plugged off, and the woman has headaches, sinusitis, "hot flashes," etc., which, repeated day after day, lead to physical and mental exhaustion or a state in which her "nerves are shot," often prompting her to seek psychiatric help. This happens at any age during her "sexual life."

The bottom line is that women who do not reach their climax consistently shouldn't have to practice sex. Whether it is for functional or organic reasons. This book contends that in most instances organic reasons prevent her from reaching her climax consistenly.

64

"HOT FLASHES"

Another subject I would like to cover is "hot flashes."
Quite often, young women ask me if they are having "hot
flashes;" they have these chills and fever, and it is my
feeling that they are having "hot flashes." I think hot
flashes occur because of swelling of the turbinates of the
nose due to many causes. Turbinates are the large pieces of
round tissue in the nose that may cause obstruction of the
openings of the sinuses that drain between them. They function primarily to swell by markedly increasing their content
of warm blood in cold weather to warm the air going over them
to the internal temperature of 98.6 that has to be maintained
at all times. Conversely, they shrink in warm weather due to
the same necessity.

This erectile tissue swells in response to several things;
noxious odors, certain allergens, etc. Whatever the cause of
the swelling, the end results are the same: The obstruction
of the discharge from the sinuses. Of course, obstruction of
the discharge from any organ in the body leads to retention
of secretions, which leads to putrefaction or inflammation
due to the changing or mutation of the natural flora of
bacteria into more virulent organisms within the organ. With
obstruction and retention of secretions, the cultural media
for mutant pathogens become ideal, and they dominate and begin
to take over in the obstructed organ. The mutant organisms
get into the blood stream. The tremendous amount of blood
supplying the area goes to all parts of the body and the individual actually gets septicemia from infected sinuses, or
"blood poisoning."

I am strongly convinced that the erectile tissue in the
turbinates responds exactly to stimuli that similarly cause
response in the female clitoris and in the male glans penis.
That is, they are composed of the same type tissue, and the
elaboration of a particular hormone from the woman or man who
has reached a climax causes an opening up of the blood vessel

valves of this erectile tissue and allows the blood to be
excreted; all of these organs shrink as if by one command at
climax. Whether this is adrenalin or not is not known, but
it acts the same way. This is why I think it is very easy for
the male to reach a subminimal climax by masturbation, etc.
However, in the female, it is extremely difficult, but it is
perhaps much more important for her to reach a climax because
of all of her body systems it affects.

It is absolutely necessary for a female to be free of all
pelvic disease in order for her to reach a climax. When she
is free of all disease, the male can insert his phallus into
her to its depth, thus enabling her to reach a maximal climax.
It is a very delicate thing for her to reach a climax, but
once she reaches this climax, an adrenalin-like hormone is
elaborated into the blood stream which causes a shrinking of
the nasal turbinates. This shrinking allows the sinuses to
drain, and there will not be obstruction, or pile-up, of
noxious bacteria in the sinuses. If the woman can have regular sex and achieve regular normal climaxes over a period of
time, then the hot flashes will not occur. Her turbinates
will not swell, and her nose will be literally "wide open,"
as the slang phrase alludes to, all the time.

The ravages of the hot flashes can occur at any age after
puberty in the female in any instance in which complete sexual
satisfaction is not achieved, particularly after the sex act
has been initiated.

However, if a young woman suffers from a female disease,
there are things that excite her to erection in her clitoris
and turbinates; for example, a male can excite her, or maybe
a movie or book or even certain movements excite her. Whatever
the occurrence, this female should be taken care of by normal
sexual climaxes, if feasible. But if she is unable to reach
a climax because of disease, or whatever, then the erectile
tissue in her turbinates continues distended, obstructing the
sinuses, and, of course, she will have an interrupted night's
sleep and perhaps sleep only one or two hours. She goes to
work, and then the next night the same thing occurs, she gets
excited but is unable to be fulfilled. Her turbinates stay
swollen, the obstruction in her sinuses become more fixed,
and infection sets in. Bacteria are disseminated into her
blood stream since there is not external egress, and the female continues to have headaches, hot and cold flashes, and
becomes extremely agitated. This same thing happens to the
female during the menopausal period. That is, she has usually
been excited by some sexual movement or something that she has
recalled, and there is little chance for her to climax. Over
a period of weeks, her turbinates become enlarged, and she
has this rush of bacteria into the blood stream, causing "hot
flashes." After a period of time, frigidity, for she has be-

come conditioned to the frustration, and would rather be beaten by a whip than allow her body to suffer the trauma of unfulfilled sexual excitement repeatedly. Indeed, she will run from one doctor's office to another for relief with tranquilizers, to the liquor store, or more expensively, to help her turbinates to shrink, street drugs. This is very frustrating, particularly at menopause, for social and family ties often make it impossible for her to achieve a normal sex outlet outside of the marriage. Her options are very limited, indeed.

Women often have the problem of "hot flashes" in middle age. They usually occur when the healthy pelvic woman has sporadic sexual copulation. These middle-aged women will usually have a middle-aged man who will participate at sparse intervals, that is, will have sex every two or three weeks. If, of course, he had sex at regular intervals, as a younger man would with his wife, then the turbinates would stay shrunken, and she would not have a sinus problem or "hot flashes." But what usually happens is that she becomes excited during these intervals, the turbinates enlarge, and she has hot and cold flashes; the middle-aged man is not only hampered by the aging process, but often his economic responsibilities are so great that they severely curtail his limited energy for he has to work excessively.

My direction to patients who have these problems is that they either have to tell the "old" man to speed it up and increase the number and regularity of sexual acts he has with the woman, or he should abstain completely. If he does this, then the ovaries completely involute, and she doesn't have the exciting problem of clitoral enlargement and, likewise, of the nasal turbinates. In any event, occasional sex or occasional climax becomes extremely nerve-racking, leading to pills and alcohol consumption, both of which probably have a component that shrinks erectile tissue at least initially-- the turbinates in the nose and the clitoris, as well as the glans penis--and these people often have no sexual desire. However, as soon as the effect of the drug or alcohol wears off, there is a rebound swelling of the nose, headaches, etc., and the patient has the typical "hangover."

Other changes come about at this age from the hysterectomizing of the woman. Quite often after the sexual lifetime, or at least twenty years of fibroids or of pelvic inflammatory disease, these hysteretomized women, with the ovaries left in, suddenly become extremely passionate, and they want sex regularly and climax for the first time in their lives.

These women usually start out at a younger age with chronic pelvic inflammatory disease as a result of an abortion or infection, fibroids, or tampons, ruptured appendix, and have a retroflexed uterus; they subsequently go from doctor to doctor with this problem. They become frigid, and unfortunately , they do not know why. Infection is usually transmitted to the husband's prostate glands or her Bartholin glands, and if she does get this cleared up and have her uterus and pelvis in a healthy condition, he will insinuate her with infection again, or the infected Bartholin glands will do the same thing. This low-grade non-veneral infection bounces back and forth until some kindly old doctor removes her female organs. After this is done, the woman will finally be able to accept the phallus with complete fulfillment if her ovary or ovaries are still there.

But, alas! The ballgame is over. The "old" man has adjusted to limited sex or no sex, or he has found other forms of tranquilization, such as alcohol, which is probably the most frequent, going out with the boys, or maybe he has found another woman who has accepted him. Or, in most instances, next to alcohol, the "old" man has readjusted his sexual desires to conform to the limited sexual desires of the infected or frigid female. Regardless of how successful extramarital relations are, they are almost never completely gratifying.

When the woman has had all of this disease removed, usually her sexual desires are quickened, and she becomes a much more aggressive sex partner and quite often tries to recapture all of the lost years, provided that at least a small segment of one of her ovaries is left in place. In any event, the problem of the woman quite often is that she becomes too aggressive; every time the man comes home, she is ready and waiting for sex; coming home becomes like going to work.

THE HYSTERECTOMIZED WOMAN AND THE MENOPAUSE

So often women do not really understand what happens to their bodies when their uterus has to be removed. Some women still allude to a partial hysterectomy, or they may say a total hysterectomy. Both terms, however, will quite often have little meaning to a woman because she will not understand what is happening to her.

For simplicity, there are two situations. One is simply hysterectomy in which the uterus is removed. The other situation, for clarity, is when the uterus is removed along with both ovaries and the tubes.

In the former instance there is little change in the female's hormone production, or if there is, it is only a few months' change in the basic physiology of the woman's hormones. In the latter instance, there is considerable change in the hormone's physiology permanently. The black woman, quite often in this instance, is a victim of a cultural difference and perhaps a pathophysiologic difference from the white woman, for she often is a victim of the latter situation.

The black woman, who suffers immeasurably more than the white woman with problems arising out of her quite enlarged uterus and the subsequent disease and suffering, often has to shop from doctor to doctor before she can find one who has the belief and convictions to buck tissue committee, etc., in the hospital and remove the uterus--that is, unless the uterus contains obvious tumors, etc.

In most instances, however, there will be some pathology noted that has caused excessive suffering socially, physically, and economically by the black female before the uterus is removed. She will suffer because so often in the frigid state in which she has found herself because of the foregoing pathology she will leave her husband, or he will channel his energy to alcohol, gambling, hunting, sports, or another woman, etc. never to return to her as sexually aggressive as he might have

69

been, regardless of whether or not the disease is removed, for he has formed another pattern of living.

It goes without saying how enormous is the effect this situation has on the children and other members of the family. Changes quite often occur during the thirties and forties of the couple's life, when the children are in their teens and early adulthood, that may account for the wildness that is often encountered in men as they reach the early forties. Quite often, when hysterectomy is done, the surgeon feels that because the ovaries have become functionless, as far as child-bearing is concerned, bilateral, oophorectomy must be done. Even though the ovaries are normal or look atrophic at the time of surgery. Ovarian cysts may form later, necessitating more future surgery; therefore, it is easier for the surgeon to remove the ovaries bilaterally and initially. Also, the ovaries are atrophic because quite often, for years, leading up to the surgical intervention for disease, they have not been stimulated by climactic sexual activity and subsequent function because the diseased woman cannot stand the complete relaxation at regular intervals to allow complete penetration of the phallus, necessary for climax and necessary for normal ovarian function.

But more important than anything, the surgeon is under the pressure of the excited woman facing surgery and is admonished to "take everything out"--"I don't want to have you go back in there for anything"--and with the good possibility that larger cysts may form in one of the ovaries or any of many possible situations may develop in the remaining ovary or ovaries, the surgeon is almost compelled to carry out the lady's wishes, particularly with the current rise in malpractice suits.

During the initial procedure, when you equate the reason for bilateral oophorectomy against not doing it at the meno-pause age, it is hard to say what to do. The facts are that changes are seen in the general health of these relatively castrated women because of existing disease; one finds these women to be constantly in the physician's office with nervous problems, chills, fever, menopausal symptoms, etc., exactly as seen after the menopause--surgical or otherwise.

The operating surgeon quite often does not have to be bothered with these complaints before or after surgery, for he has simply turned the complaining woman back over to the internist or general practitioner, who struggles along trying to plug up the holes with hormone pills, vaginal hormone creams, bushels of nerve pills, etc., all of which are prescribed by the primary care physician and all are quite often relatively ineffective and effective only for short intervals.

A syndrome of symptoms is often noted in women who have had surgical menopause unlike any that I have ever seen, in which the women often presents herself to emergency room

complaining of dizziness, hot flashes, and tachycardia which
often increases to the point that the patient winds up in the
emergency room with P.V.C.'s (Ventricular premature beats)
which often are accompanied by vertigo and can lead to syncope
or ventricular fibrillation and cardiac arrest which can follow
unless treated appropriately. The upshot is that women in this
condition often have to adjust the amount of estrogen hormone
needed for their particular needs. Some women complain that
when they take too much, they feel like they want to rape
someone. Of course, when they don't take enough, they have
the foregoing symptoms to a lesser degree.

The unfortunate ones who can't take any hormones because
of cancer, recurrent deep phlebitis, hypertension, heart disease, etc., really have to rely on tranquillizers and other
medicines to plug up the "holes" of their symptoms.

In the meantime, there is not a normal sexual relationship as far as the husband is concerned, for the castrated
woman, surgically or otherwise, finds it hard to reach a
climax, it seems, and he is quite often worse off sexually
than he was before the hysterectomy and bilateral salpingo-
oophorectomy. What is to be done with these women who suffer
in silence? I do not know.

The confusion arises, I believe, during the years leading
up to the hysterectomy. The woman with the diseased pelvis
was not able to reach a climax because she could not relax
sufficiently. Unfortunately, this situation, with all the
"hot flashes," etc., may start when the young woman, particularly with a diseased pelvis, first begins to have sex, and
her whole sex life from fifteen to sixty is filled with "hot
flashes," and thus, misery for herself, her children, and
particularly her husband, for she, too, is like a "spayed
cat." So many young women in their late teens have infected
abortions, which lead to chronic salpingitis, tumors, tubal
pregnancy, sterility, adenomyosis and, most important, subsequent frigidity and "hot flashes." If, for some reason, after
twenty to thirty years of suffering, she has a complete
hysterectomy, with one ovary left behind, she will feel like
a new woman, or as one preacher's wife told me after the foregoing surgery and removal of diseased tumors, with one ovary
left behind, that if she had known sex was as good as it was
to her after surgery, she would have had the surgery done as
a teenager.

There are certain reasons why women lose their husbands
by divorce or separation before and after hysterectomies. One
reason, I believe, is that such a woman quite often has been
spayed before surgery by infection secondary to tumors, retroflexion, etc., and like the spayed cat and dog, she has no
desire for males. She can't tolerate the extreme repeated
agitation of the excitement stage of sex with repeated inability

to climax and the subsequent letdown of "hot flashes" for days afterward. Other reasons are, as I alluded to before, that the man had to make other social adjustments, particularly with another woman during the long years before the hysterectomy, when the wife was for all practical purposes functionally "spayed" by the disease and tumors she had that finally led to her hysterectomy. If the ovaries, undiseased, are left in place, the woman becomes so sexually demanding that the man often cannot make the adjustment to her as she is now from the other woman, alcohol, drugs, etc., fast enough to satisfy her and she divorces him. If, however, the ovaries are completely removed, it gives the wayward, sexually potent husband an excuse to do what he has been desirous of doing for years, and he will "file for a divorce." In some instances, the husband continues to drink himself into bad health; both the husband and the spayed wife then become, for all practical purposes, "spayed" together.

Other factors at this age, such as the lack of fear of pregnancy, and the removal of the disease, except, of course, at least one ovary, now allow her to reach a climax and give the woman a new freedom, a new sexual aggressiveness. There is now no challenge for the man; he loses interest, and his mind and eyes begin to roam for newer and quite often greener pastures or hills to conquer, if he is not already committed. Often, it may be better that the woman tell the husband that she has not had a hysterectomy, that there is a remote possibility of pregnancy and she should go through a monthly five-day period of pseudomenstruation so that the "old man" can recharge his batteries, as in God's original master plan, particularly with his diminishing libido, fear of aging, and inability to "cut the mustard." The older man will often try a younger woman, who is usually more aggressive sexually than older women. She can become pregnant easier, more problems for the masochistic male. Also, she reaches a climax easier, and her "heat" may be higher. In addition, with the "tighter" introitus, the younger woman may excite a more complete emptying of the older male's prostate by a stronger contraction of the muscle around the prostate gland, emptying not only more prostatic fluid but also often emptying the product of chronic prostatic infection, which had been dormant for years. This makes room for regrowth of parenchymal tissue, and increases his libido. Unfortunately, quite often, this occurs at the expense of the younger woman, who incurs pelvic infection, particularly if her organs are out of place, etc.

It has been a policy of mine to tell the hysterectomized woman with at least one ovary that she should make these adjustments to her new increased libido by restraining herself from trying to enjoy her sexual appetite almost to the point of turning her husband "off" sex.

For a man is like the kid that has trees of "delicious" apples in his own back yard, but the old crabapple tree in the neighbor's yard is always better, particularly if he has to steal them. This is essentially what happens psychologically in the above instances, and quite often this does lead to complications, and sometimes divorce. Therefore, I tell the black woman to continue to play the game of life after surgery, menses, pregnancy, etc. with her husband, although I do believe that the psychological aspect, where sex is concerned, is very minimal, indeed.

Of course, the woman must have adequate sex at regular intervals, perhaps two to three times per week if she is to escape the ravages of the recurring menopause, a condition that I feel represents temporary involution of the ovaries, for sex and climax is the stimulus for ovarian activity, and sexual abstinence causes involution and consequent "hot flashes" etc., only to have the ovaries restimulated when the female gets into a satisfying and regular sexual relationship.

Essentially the involutional changes going on in the ovary causes menopausal symptoms, due to the lack of regular sex and regular climaxing. Only in the latter instances can the ovary release the ingredients necessary to prevent the ravages of the "minnies"--headaches, dizziness, evil disposition, etc. Thus, these "hot flashes" are seen in young women filled with disease who are stimulated by their partner but can't relax enough to climax. The same type of menopausal changes occur with women in their forties through sixties, who are still able to enjoy normal, regular sex with a satisfactory climax, then for some reason their climax outlet stops, or their spouse dies, etc., then they have to go through the "change." Unfortunately, as the female gets older, the problematic possibilities of all of the ingredients for normal frequent climax arriving at the same time are reduced. The ovary's blood supply is not good, her pelvic ligaments are calcified, particularly the sacroiliac ones, and the one at the symphysis pubis also becomes calcified, the number of capable effective lovers diminishes, etc., and quite often she will go through the few months of the "minnies." As the infirmities of aging progress, the problematic possibilities of compatible sexual climax between two people is reduced progressively; the man dies, becomes impotent, gets "tired," gets prostate cancer, or starts wandering away from home. And the woman will quite often not allow herself to become involved or stimulated for she does not want to go through the trauma of the "letdown" of the "minnies" again.

In instances in which women who have practiced the act of sex regularly and then suddenly have occasional sex encounters, for example, a widow who has sex every four to six months, the female goes through the same changes as the ovar-ectomized woman or the "menopausal" woman, with headaches, dizziness, blurring of vision, tiredness, etc., after each sexual encounter and soon they become "turned off" by sex. Interestingly enough, menopausal-age women with a very normal pelvis are very capable sexually, usually with younger lovers and have no hot flashes, etc.; they do not go through these changes, and they go on into their seventies, etc., fully enjoying sex without the foregoing ravages of menopause or "hot flashes," as long as they have climaxes regularly. This may account for the fact that once a woman has indulged in sex at any age, in order not to be ravaged by these little "minnies," she must continue to participate regularly. Indeed, this may account for the apple that Eve ate. For she had to continue to participate in sex. The hormone pills and shots are prescribed to increase the female hormone level, but more and more women are turning them down. Quite often, I wonder whether or not implanting the ovary or a small part of the resected ovary into the abdominal wall musculature would not be a wise idea indeed, when hysterectomy and bilateral salpingo-oophorectomy have to be done. Also, I wonder whether or not there should be some form of ovarian homoplant transplanted into the abdominal wall musculature from a compatible donor in those instances in which the ovaries have to be removed because of cancer, etc. I do not believe that we have scratched the surface as to the physical and social ramifica-tions of the ovary and its function other than in childbearing. On the other hand, menopausal-aged women who lose their mates suddenly and do not participate any more in sex will have, in three to six months, severe attacks of the "minnies," and then they are bothered no more unless they have an occasional sexual relationship, and then they have to go through the same slowing down of their ovaries all over again with each occasional encounter. The same, of course, happens to women of any age; however, the younger the woman, the higher the probability that she will run into a man to satisfy her sexual needs more often. And the easier it is for her ovaries to rebound and function normally after the temporary involution they go through after prolonged abstinence.

One unusual aspect of the menopause is the beginning ossification of the symphysis pubis and the sacroiliac joints, "potential joints" during active sexual life, which open up to allow the baby's head to be accommodated during childbirth under stimulation of a hormone, Relaxin. More on this later.

Another unusual aspect of the "minnies" is that there is often an increased susceptibility to "coids" perhaps due to the inter-relationship that erectile tissue of the genital tract has with the turbinates in the nose, causing them to swell when aroused by erotic stimulation. The swollen turbinates close off the egress of the sinuses, whose openings are controlled by their swelling and diminution of swelling. When a male or female reaches a climax, an adrenalin-like material is elaborated, the turbinates shrink, the sinus openings are consequently increased in size, and the sinuses drain. The individual feels as though his or her nose has been opened. In any event, they breathe easier and are able to relax, become euphoric, without the usual tension headaches seen when climax is not reached. And finally stagnated infected drainage from the sinuses is seen--the "head cold."

Men, and particularly women, who do not reach a climax after an erotic interplay usually find that the turbinates remain enlarged and engorged; thus, the sinuses are closed off, and the following day they have a terrific headache, chills, fever, etc., or "hot flashes." Women who have been spayed or women who have many pelvic infections or for any reason cannot reach a climax seem to continue in a perpetual state of swollen turbinates and subsequent headaches, with chills and fever due to stagnated pus in the sinuses; exogenous hormones for some reason seem to relieve the castrated woman of this malady temporarily.

Some women describe "hot flashes" as chills and fever like a "hot poker" running up and down their backs. Other descriptions are that they feel like running outside in the cold air with their clothes off. Quite often these attacks occur when the woman is in an erotic situation, in cases in which orgiastic rhythms arouse a certain eroticism, or when a particularly attractive man comes on the scene. I believe that these attacks occur when the female is excited but cannot reach a climax, especially if she has been spayed, pathologically or surgically. That is, she is in a perpetual state of eroticism with little or no chance for release. There seems to be a hormone released when the woman reaches a climax that reduces the ravages of these "hot flashes," particularly if she is able to climax at regular intervals.

But what usually happens to these women that are hysterectomized is that they are just below the menopause age or around the menopause age; in spite of the fact that you may leave the ovaries in, they begin to have "hot flashes" and these will go on over a period of several weeks or even several months, after surgery, because of lack of sex during the healing state, or at least they are afraid to relax for several months even after the pain leaves--no relaxation, no climax. Then it depends on whether or not they are "reactivated" with a healthy sex partner afterwards. I believe that an adequate healthy sexual intercourse, with a good climax to stimulate the ovaries to produce an adrenalin-like hormone material, in turn reduces the "hot flashes." It is this climax that causes the woman to finally begin to enjoy sexual inter-

course if it is done regularly, even to the point that she
enjoys it so much that every time the man comes home, her
legs "flop open." Then it can begin to be a job for the man;
it is like getting too much ice cream; he can become bored with
it, particularly if he has had to make an adjustment outside
for several years before his wife's surgery. It seems that
life has to have a challenge. This is essentially what happens
psychologically in these instances, and quite often this leads
to complications and even divorce. Although this is the other
side of the coin, and the woman is perfectly normal after
hysterectomy, if one or more ovaries are left in place, I tell
the black woman to continue to "play the game" after surgery
with her husband, to allow a five-day abstinence once each
month to simulate the menstral period, to complain of being
"tired," even though she may be as "hot as a firecracker,"
or ultimately to tell him that she can get pregnant. This
latter, of course, when you invoke professional privileged
information and tell the husband only that the "tumors have
been removed," when hysterectomy is done; of course, the
wife, the patient, should know the whole truth.

One unusual aspect of the menopause in women is the beginning calcifications of the sacroiliac joints through whose
orifices nerves to the legs and thighs pass which, during active sexual life, have fibrinous bridges and are classified as
potential joints that open to accommodate the head of the baby
during delivery. These become fused with calculus deposits
if they are not used often. And with fusion, calcification and
inflammation form in the joints, particularly when the thighs
are not pushed apart at regular intervals, as during frequent
climaxes. Therefore, the woman who has occasional sex, particularly around menopause age, will have her legs pushed
open hard at the moment of climax, thus producing referred
spasms to the thigh muscles or "charley horses" down the side,
or lateral, aspect of the thighs as the calcific deposits tear
into the nerves coming through the affected sacroliac orifices
to supply innervation to the affected muscles. This, of course,
cuts off the climax, and quite often it interferes with the
male climax, a source of considerable embarrassment to the female, because what has happened to her is that the sacroiliac
joint, like the symphsis pubis, is a "potential joint" and has
now become calcified and relatively fixed, almost to the point
where it becomes like another bone. Now, in addition to
"opening up" during the act of having a baby, to accommodate
the baby's head, being stimulated by the hormone, Relaxin, this
joint has a tendency to be involved when the thighs are
physically and roughly abducted or pushed apart near climax,
causing a breaking up of the new calcium that has been deposited
in these joints following long periods, whenever baby production is down or climax reaching is down, particularly during

the years around the menopause. This breaking up of the calcium spicules, like icicles, pushes them into the spinal nerves
supplying the leg muscles, which come out of holes in the lateral aspect of the vertebrae. When these nerves are agitated
by the broken calcific spicules, the innervated muscles go
into a tonic type of spasm, and it is this spasm that causes
the pain, reflected in the patient's mind as "charley horses,"
in the lateral aspect of the thigh. And over the months and
years, if she continues to have sex regularly and continues to
be roughly abducted, thighs pushed out, after an interval,
she will reach a climax--this situation will clear up. But
if she has sex only at occasional intervals, then the condition of "charley horses" will be repeated with each act of
sex and, of course, here again the mind becomes conditioned
to the fact that at that moment she will have this type of
pain, and instead of concentrating on the climax or trying
to reach the climax, the woman concentrates on the pain that
she contemplates and the subsequent embarrassment. She
cannot relax, and the magic seconds of climax pass her by.
This, of course, will lead to frigidity and abstinence by the
normal female after a period of time, and she, too, becomes
functionally spayed, although here, also, pelvic inflammatory
disease and aging seems to accelerate the condition.

In addition to the menopausal changes that the unclimaxed
woman has the next day, there is a blurring of vision, dizziness, etc., and the woman's nerves will be blown as far as
trying sex again, for her mind has become conditioned to the
possibility of hurting again at the moment of climax, and for
weeks and months afterward she will approach that moment with
some trepidation. However, with repeated exercise, sexual and
physical, the sacroiliac joint will relax, and the legs can
be opened widely again if the act is done repeatedly, and other
systems, ovaries, etc., are ready.

Another fact about the hysterectomized woman is the lack of
fear of having children. This is a fear that quite often
before hysterectomy leads to "coitus interruptus," the unde-
sirable situation of having to stop before ejaculation. This,
of course, results in symptoms in the woman similar to the
menopause; after the act, she remains excited and restless.
The following day, she is agitated, dizzy, nervous, headachy,
etc.

In addition, the following types of contraception may
also have made her sexual life rather miserable during the
childbearing period, if she had to use a douche to keep from
getting pregnant. The condom was often painful to the sides
of the vagina, plus the fear of it bursting is another psychological reason why the woman would often not enjoy sex to
its fullest. Birth control pills and the intrauterine device
have not given the universal relief physically, ecstatically,

or psychologically that we might have expected. Usually, at the age of forty or fifty, the woman may become free of the fear of childbearing, or she has had a hysterectomy with retention of her ovaries. In either instance, it frees her inhibitions so that she can relax completely, and at this time she becomes a real "tiger." The male often has had to sublimate himself sexually for years and may become an impotent "mouse," particularly if he has remained a "good guy" and has allowed alcohol to nudge him and tranquilize him nightly. The impotence, of course, is a sequel not only of impaired liver function from alcohol, with its inability to reduce estrogen levels in the blood, but the man may also have formed a life pattern of sublimating his sexual desires by exercise, adultery, "pot" smoking, etc., all of which may be hard to change.

Actually, what the whole thing is about is having babies. And God, in his infinite wisdom, has made it so that the more you enjoy the act, the greater your climax, the greater the chance for pregnancy, and man, in his infinite wisdom, has not scratched the surface in turning the situation around.

In a situation of whether to hysterectomize or not to hysterectomize, I am firmly convinced that in the years prior to the menopause age, which is perhaps the ages of thirty to fifty-five, there is a considerable amount of disease built up in the female as a result of pregnancy and retroflexion of the uterus, and perhaps even as a result of the male's prostatitis. In all instances, the prime factor causing most of the problems, other than fibroids, in black females particularly, is the retroflexion of the uterus and the subsequent infection in her tubes and ovaries. Both situations cause stagnation of secretions to the point that the patient's own normal flora of bacteria, particularly from the anus, begin to infect her by mutation and increased virulence and destroy her sexually by abscess formation, particularly in her tubes, etc., when the bacteria are confined to the relatively closed organs for a protracted period.

What this does essentially is to make the woman, over a period of years, frigid. This is a gradual process, and it is not noticed by the woman or her husband. She becomes frigid because of the conditioning of her mind. She is unable to reach a climax through the conditioning brought about by the painful sex act to the point that it becomes an extremely nerve-racking situation for her. She is almost to the point of climax but cannot achieve it because of the pain or contemplated pain, and then the man copulates and she cannot relax enough to allow her body to benefit by the enlarging phallus. It is a situation in which the female becomes extremely agitated. In order for the female to reach a climax, there has to be a symphony, a concert, between the split-

second act of copulation between the male and female. But she
cannot do this because of the fear of the enlarging phallus
and her subsequent tightening up of the vaginal muscles and
thigh muscles to prevent the enlarging phallus from being
thrust too far into her, thus causing much damage to infected
or inflamed organs. She is, therefore, never satisfied and
often becomes agitated by the husband and is desirous of more
sex at that instant with the hope that she can be fulfilled,
but she usually can't be.

The damage, of course, is brought about by the differences
often between the length of the phallus, which is 6-10 inches,
and the length of the vagina, which is 1.5-3 inches at the
most, and the pushing of the female's internal organs perhaps
up to a half a foot into her visceral cavity by the pounding
phallus. Of course, if the abscesses are there it is easy
to see how she will contract her muscles and her thighs in order
to prevent too much of this movement into her and the bursting
of the abscesses in her tubes.

If she is to have a normal relationship, she must be able
to allow the total entrance of the available phallus into her
to its "hilt." This entrance of the phallus to its "hilt"
allows her to climax. If she can't, the woman becomes frigid,
and, interestingly enough, the husband is later affected, also.
He becomes either impotent due to excessive alcohol, drugs,
or what have you, or he finds another woman to compensate
for his wife's inability to have normal sex with him. The
infected wife often subtly encourages this type of relationship by the male even to the point where she subtly allows
alcohol excess or philandering so that she can hold on to her
man, yet not have to be punished by excessive sex acts that
tranquilize the man, as alcohol does, but only punishes the
woman who cannot climax. Sex for this woman is like having
to be beaten by a "rubber hose."

The tranquilization of the man by alcohol may work initially, but gradually his intake is increased more and more
until quite often he becomes an alcoholic, and the same happens
with drugs. In many instances, the man begins to divert his
attention to younger women, who are able to have relatively
excessive sex with him. He is usually financially able around
menopause to afford sex with younger women; quite often, if he
hasn't punished his body too much with alcohol or drugs, he
can have a fair and adequate sexual relationship with younger
woman or another healthy woman.

This is the age in which the middle-aged woman begins
to lose her man. Of course, the fights and arguments that
occur prior to this disruption make it quite easy for her to
adjust to the loss of her long-time paramour, especially if
the disease process continues. Enter the surgeon, who will
operate on the individual female patient. If he does a

hysterectomy alone and removes the diseased organs yet leaves one ovary, actually what he leaves is a woman, usually, with a considerable amount of sexual capabilities; she becomes extremely demanding, sexually, even to the point that she becomes quite loose with her husband. This is another reason why she may lose her husband at this stage in the marriage. The other reason is that if the surgeon does "spay" the woman, not only is her sexual capability reduced, but also she has all the other anxieties that affected her before the diseased organs were removed.

There are reasons for the surgeon to remove the female's ovaries; there are medical reasons--the fear of cancer, for example, developing in a "hidden organ"--for there is no sure and easy way to check even at the time of surgery, whether cancer is or is not present. There is the necessity of re-moving the ovary when the diseased tubes are removed; otherwise, the blood supply to the ovaries is compromised, and the pos-sibility of ovarian cysts is increased. Both of these may be sources of embarrassment to the surgeon later. But, more than anything else, the female will usually have suffered for so long and become so frigid that often she has lost her husband, or she is in the process of divorcing him, whom she has subtly sent down the street to alcohol, drugs, or other sex. There-fore, she entreats the surgeon to "take it all out." With medico-legal problems as they are, the surgeon has no alter-native--and to turn her around at this stage of the game by leaving an ovary in may be more disruptive, anyway, to the new pattern of life to which she and her husband both have become adapted. Also, the possibility of ovarian and breast cancer seems to increase at this age.

If the ovaries are for some reason removed in this type of situation, the woman's pattern of living continues pretty much undisturbed, as well as the husband's, who has already made the adjustment that he isn't going to have much sex anymore with this wife. The female, by being spayed, has little sexual desire, for without the ovaries, only on rare occasions can she reach a climax. She becomes passionate, but without a climax regularly, sex begins to blow her mind. In fact, it becomes tortuous for her to become "hot" with no possible relief. Whatever situation the man and woman have fallen into at this time makes it much easier for the adjustment, when the woman is spayed, at least on the surface. However, with the knowledge that this is what is happening to her, the black woman can probably compensate for the new situation that she faces if her ovaries are left in place at hysterectomy. Under those circumstances, sex becomes a tremendous outlet for her anxieties, and if she plays the game right and does not let him know what the surgeon has removed, the husband can get into the act, too, if it is not too late and his liver and psyche are not too far gone due to alcoholism, etc. A woman with ovaries removed, of course, often does not have the pain she associated with intercourse before her surgery.

I believe that the God-given or natural balance between the healthy man and the healthy woman should be simulated as closely as possible if they are to continue to have a healthy sexual relationship. I feel that the man, over a period of months or perhaps years, will stop his drinking, his liver will get better, his potency will improve, and they can go on into old age with a very healthy and beautiful family relationship.

However, if the man cannot or does not straighten up from alcohol, philandering, etc., and become sexually aggressive to the hysterectomized female, with an ovary or ovaries intact, she will usually be the aggressor in divorce, dumping the husband for a more viable sexual partner, for she becomes not only agitated mentally but physically, also, by inadequate and nerve-racking performance by her mate. If she has been spayed, of course, there is usually no satisfying her sexually or otherwise, regardless, and these individuals are usually doomed also to divorce. Unfortunately, this situation occurs too often among blacks.

What we are dealing with here is a situation in which man actually involves the whole family, not only the female and the male but also the children. Indeed, on a large scale, it involves society, particularly the black people, because the male and female begin to have discord (and certainly our females, who have a considerable amount of trouble with their female organs) leading to more and more anxiety, bickering, cutting, fighting, and more divorcing. The child without father-- again, I reiterate--has very little chance, particularly the male child, of developing any type of individuality. For he often hears his divorced mother, whom he loves more than anyone on earth, berate his father whom he looks like more than anyone else. Little wonder that our black male youth do as well as they do. Not only does sexual discord lead to a massive amount of unsocial behavior by blacks, who are otherwise, by basic genealogy and nature, some of the finest and nicest and perhaps least antisocial or antiferocious of all groups of people, but it also leads to disruption of the whole nation, for it affects all races of people.

I'm not quite clear on the use of external hormones to enhance climax in older women and simulate ovarian function. I do feel, however, that no amount of extrinsic hormone can replace the integrated split-second demand-need of a particular hormone, demanded by the body at a particular time, and in a particular amount--as from the ovary. Just as no amount of extrinsic insulin can substitute for the automatic release of insulin by the pancreas. Theoretically, when bilateral oophorectomy has to be done, strong consideration should be given to placing a very small slice of the ovary into the rectus muscle; by doing so, I really believe that the unknown hormonal effects of the ovary can be sustained by the individual woman, yet the surgeon does not have the fear of leaving cancer behind or of the possible formation of an ovarian cyst. The foregoing should be done only if the surgeon cannot possibly save the ovaries. I really believe it would help the female as she goes into middle age, certainly, and as she goes into old age, because I think some functions of the ovary have not yet been discovered.

As the female goes into the older age group, there is very little to add to the functioning of the ovaries except they certainly help prevent the osteoporosis of aging, which helps reduce the possibility of hip bone fracture, in the older woman, which is a major cause of death.

The surgeon who operates on the diseased pelvis due to fibroids, etc., and tries to preserve ovaries often hears from the female, "take everything out." In the light of this, and in the light of the fact that the woman already has been through the adjustment of having been literally spayed for years due to disease, a situation in which she has often lost her spouse, or he has turned to "chippy chasing" or alcohol drinking or drug taking or other ways to suppress his natural sexual drive, you have compensatory adjustment in the relationship to the relatively spayed woman already in motion. To not surgically spay the woman when the fibroid uterus is removed would only upset the very sensitive balance between the man and woman and her peculiar situation at the particular time, which, in itself, can cause considerable problems. For the male to have to give up his "chippy chasing" or to try to readjust an alcoholic into trying to become potent again has to be considered as insurmountable problems, or, by the time the new adjustment is made it takes too long. Therefore, spaying the woman often allows her to continue in her adjusted siutation; unfortunately for her at this time, it is often one in which there has been no potent man for years, for sex has turned her off. Indeed, some women go through a lifetime, have children, and maintain marriage without ever having reached a meaningful climax because of intercurrent pelvic disease and the conditioning of her mind between intervals of pelvic problems.

In the early years of marriage, the excessively energetic black male often has difficulty making adjustments to the problems of the black female and the sexual frustrations they may run into, particularly when she has problems. On the other hand, the black female will quite often have her children and other things that will keep her quite well occupied and leave the black male, to a certain extent, up to his own divertisement, and the greatest divertisement that the black man has is

82

alcohol, in this monogamous country, to keep him from bothering his subtly progressing frigid spouse as the fibroids continue to grow and cause chronic infection.

Usually after the first baby, changes occur in the female organs sexually which consequently affect the young black male. The sequence of events is that the excessively sexual young black male has a reduced outlet for his aggressions. He knows that he can't have sex, so he drinks or smokes "pot" initially to become tranquilized, for he has to "meet the man" the next morning. As his tolerance increases, so does his inability to "meet the man." More lost time, more need for money to take care of his increasing habit. Stealing becomes necessary; more agitation because of less money at home. Divorce follows; more stealing until finally he is caught and imprisoned. Thus there is an excessively high number of young black males incarcerated in jails all over the country. A good amount of this problem can be traced back directly to drugs and frustrated sexual outlets.

He will take a considerable amount of alcohol and drugs. If he manages to get over the mid-thirties and early forties without going to jail, usually, he will enter into a middle-aged phase to a certain extent, with a pretty good adjustment to the sexual situation because his liver is perhaps fibrotic by this time due to the chemical reaction of alcohol and drugs, so that his liver has a marked reduction in its ability to handle the estrogens in his body, and he becomes impotent. It is a known fact that both sexes have male and female hormones that allow a certain relatively higher level of the male hormone, testosterone, in males, which keep the male a little bit more male and more potent. As the liver becomes destroyed, due to the poisoning effects of alcohol particularly, there is less tissue available to detoxify the estrogen, so that its relative level to testosterone is markedly increased, thus reducing the potency of the black male and the desire for sex because his phallus will no longer become erect.

In any event, as the man approaches middle age, usually the frigid black woman and now-impotent black male will make an adjustment to their diseases, together with sex, after years of progressive sexual frigidity, frustration, impotency and disease.

If the woman with years of infection and frigidity has a hysterectomy, and both ovaries are removed, now impotent or unfaithful, the husband and wife are compatible, and they continue on with their lives undisturbed. If the ovaries are not removed, this leaves a sexually healthy woman who can tolerate the erect phallus and can now tolerate it better than ever; perhaps because of the ovaries remaining, she becomes sexually aggressive. By this, I mean she is no longer bothered with tumors and infections and can relax completely and appreciate the entire length of the available phallus. This relaxation on her part is achieved by the lack of fear of pregnancy, the lack of fear of disease and pain, the lack of displaced organs, the ability to relax totally and achieve climax, and perhaps the knowledge that she is being seduced each time, perhaps for the last time, as she grows older.

The adrenal glands, which produce male and female hormones, can compensate for the foregoing, but they are not as effective as the primary hormone producers, the ovaries and testes.

A man's desire to continue to drink is quite often encouraged by his subsequent failure to become potent with the hysterectomized but not oophorectomized woman. That is, at the moment he is called on by this vitalized female to have sex, mentally, he has been so frustrated by her frigidity in the past that he is reluctant to stop "sucking on the bottle" for fear that this new woman may only be a temporary thing, and he will again be frustrated in sex, as has happened so often in the past. There has to be a sort of natural rhythm between sex partners which, in itself, is difficult for both parties to be ready at the same time over a protracted period of years--true love? Or at least, true sex love, which may be different than what we have been programmed into thinking of over the years.

Other things begin to happen as the woman begins to enter into the menopause. Quite often, in the process of having sex, she will try to reach a climax, and at the moment of climax, her legs are pushed outward or she actually pushes them apart herself to reach that point. As mentioned previously, at that moment, she begins to have a "charley horse." Her legs begin to cramp, and she begins to hurt excruciatingly. She becomes very embarrassed by this type of reaction. This, of course, leads to the inability to reach a climax and considerable frustration.

Infection in the male prostate is an important factor in the propagating of infection between the man and the woman because quite often many patients will have considerable treatment, only to go back to the man who shoots the same, perhaps more virulent, pus into the woman and cleanses his gland into her organs, and she has symptoms again, particularly if her organs remain abnormally positioned.

This discharge and bursting of the abscess allow the rejuvenation in the male because more prostate glandular tissue can then return. This glandular tissue is primarily involved in the production of the male sexual secretions which enhances potency. Therefore, you see older men attracted by younger women, and in the days of yore, this is the way the old kings and lords, etc., achieved rejuvenation of their potency, by cutting young girls out of the tribe, having sex with them, and subsequently finding that their nature was increased considerably.

CONCLUSION

Over the years, the superiority of one race over the other has been debated by bigots espousing their views on both sides. Some of this may have been brought about by the emphasis on evolution rather than adaptation. If the evolutionary process has taken place, it probably evolved over millions of years rather than thousands of years. Today, with all of the hundred of thousands of animals known to man, I have never heard of one changing or evolving naturally from one species or genus to another in the span of written history.

On the other hand, animals adapt to their environment, and adaptation, to me, is a more plausible and obvious short-term concept. Not only did man adapt to his particular environment as he moved toward or away from the equator from around the Black Sea, his common origin. The sun was the dominant factor, with subsequent change of color, etc., but within the scope of a short time, the races of man will probably change again, all without any discernible evolutionary rumble. This time the change will be on the basis of the increased pollution of the body by the atmosphere, food, etc.

The young married couple often starts out very happy. Shortly after the first baby, and often in black women because they are so closely built, the Bartholin glands, etc., become chronically infected by local bacteria usually with retro-flexion of the uterus. The woman then becomes frigid.

The young black male's sex outlet is cut off. He will start drinking or smoking a joint or two initially, for he knows full well that he will not be able to have sex, or if he has it, he literally has to "rape" his wife. Therefore, subtly he delves deeper and deeper into drugs until his body becomes more and more tolerant of them. Soon, only the "hard" stuff satisfies him. By this time, he and his wife are arguing or fighting; he is missing more time from work; his habit is becoming more expensive; he loses his job, and before long, he has to resort to stealing to support his habit. With his self-respect gone, he becomes a liability to society in many ways.

His male children, without the guidance of the father, also become liabilities to society. Indeed, habits and demeanors develop in the child and the child's progeny that will take many generations to change or abate completely.

> And Cain talked to Abel his brother: and
> it came to pass, when they were in the fields,
> that Cain rose up against Abel his brother, and
> slew him.
> And the Lord said unto Cain, Where is Abel
> thy brother? And he said, I know not: Am I my
> brother's keeper?

The black man's genealogy leads to, psychologically, independent or solo endeavors that are less effective economically for gain than that of the white man, who, genealogically, has been programmed for survival by joining forces with each other because of the long, barren, hard winter when cooperation with neighbors was absolute. This joining of forces has been perpetuated and, at times, prostituted by institutions; for example, kingdoms, dictatorships, and religious sects. This made it easier for the whites to fall in line, or else. Even in situations in which they had grave doubts to its morality; for example, in certain racial situations in Western culture in which they automatically close ranks. Because of this, masses of whites can be enslaved industrially without the "chains" and "fetters" that were an absolute must for the blacks here in America.

Masses of whites will go to battle, as in World War I and World War II, as if by a single command. Indeed, as the group becomes more organized, it becomes very much more susceptible to mass destruction, as was seen during World War II in the recent enslavement and annihilation of the Jews, one of the most highly organized and "close knit" groups in Western culture. Their allowing this to happen remains one of the enigmas of modern man.

Therefore, the black man, who has always responded as an individual, perhaps, in the long run, will not be any worse off than any other group.

> And the Lord God caused a deep sleep to fall
> upon Adam, and he slept: and he took one of his
> ribs, and closed up the flesh instead thereof;
> And the rib, which the Lord God had taken
> from man, made he into a woman, and brought her
> unto the man.
> And Adam said, This is now bone of my bone,
> and flesh of my flesh: She shall be called Woman,
> because she was taken out of Man.

Therefore shall a man leave his father and
his mother, and shall cleave unto his wife: and
they shall be one flesh. And they were both naked,
the man and his wife, and were not ashamed.

GLOSSARY

ABDUCT: To draw away from the median plane of the body or
     one of its parts.
ABSCESSED TUBES: See pyosalpinx.
ADAPTATION: In biology, the ability of an organism to adjust
     to a change in environment.
ADAPTATIVE: Able to adapt.
ADENOMYOSIS: Benign invasive growth of the endometrium into
     the muscular layer of the uterus.
ANTHROPOID PELVIS: A female pelvis being long and narrow.
ANUS: The outlet of the rectum.
ARTHRITIC SPICULES: Needle-shaped fragments of bone with
     arthritis.
ATROPHIC: Marked by atrophy; the reduction in size of a
     structure after having come to full functioning maturity;
     that is, atrophy of ovary during menopause.
AUTOMATIC RESPONSE: Spontaneous action or behavior without
     conscious purpose or knowledge.
BACTEREMIA: Bacteria in the blood.
BARTHOLIN GLANDS: Two small reddish-yellow bodies on either
     side of the vaginal orifice that secrete a colorless
     lubricant that bathes the vagina during sexual inter-
     course.
BLOOD POISONING: A vague term usually used to indicate the
     presence of large numbers of bacteria in the circulating
     blood.
BUFFER: A substance tending to offset reaction of an agent
     administered in conjunction with it.
CALCIFIC SPICULES: Needle-shaped fragments of calcified bone.
CALCIFICATION: Deposits of lime salts in the tissues and
     commonly in bone.
CALCULUS: An abnormal stony mass in the body.
CARNIVOROUS: Flesh eating.
CATALYST: An agent that speeds up the rate of a chemical
     reaction.

CELLULAR: Pertaining to, composed of, or derived from cells.

CEREBRAL CORTEX: Thin surface layer of gray matter of the cerebral hemispheres.

CEREBRUM: Largest part of the brain consisting of two hemispheres separated by a deep longitudinal fissure.

CERVIX: Neck of the uterus.

CAESARIAN SECTION: Removal of the fetus by means of an incision into uterus, usually by way of abdominal wall.

CHARLEY HORSE: A pulled muscle, intramuscular bleeding, torn muscle fibers.

CHRONIC INFECTION: Prolonged infection.

CLIMACTERIC: Female menopause.

CLIMAX: Period of greatest intensity; the orgasm.

COHABITATION: Living together as man and wife without being legally married.

COITUS: Sexual intercourse between man and woman.

COLON: The large intestine from the end of the ileum and beginning with the cecum to the anus.

CONDOM: A thin, flexible sheath worn over the penis, used as contraceptive device and to help prevent venereal disease.

CONGENITAL CYSTS: Cysts present at birth resulting from abnormal development.

COPULATION: Sexual intercourse.

CORPUS: The principal part of any organ; any mass or body.

CORPUS LUTEUM: Yellow body formed by the Graafian follicle that has discharged its ovum. The word luteum means yellow.

CORTEX: Outer layer of an organ as distinguished from the inner medulla.

CORTICAL: Pertains to cortex.

CULTURE MEDIA: A substance on which microorganisms may grow.

DARWINISM: The theory of biological evolution (origin of species) through natural selection.

DECEREBRATE: A person or animal who has been subjected to decerebration (removal of the brain or cutting the spinal cord at the level of the brain stem).

DECORTICATION: The removal of the surface layer of an organ or structure, as the removal of the capsule of a kidney or outer brain covering.

DEEP PHLEBITIS: Inflammation (deep) of a vein.

DIAPHRAGM: A rubber or plastic cup that fits over the cervix uteri and is used for contraceptive purposes.

DILATATION AND EFFACEMENT: Expansion of an orifice with a dilator as the head in delivery, completed--the end of labor.

DISTENSOR: Object that would cause distention (to stretch out or to become inflated).

DORMANT: In resting state; inactive.

E. COLI: Gram-negative, nonspore-forming motile bacillus

almost constantly present in the alimentary canal of
humans and some animals.

ECSTATIC: State of being exhiliarated; exulted delight.

EJACULATION: Ejection of the seminal fluids from the male
urethra.

ENDOMETRIOSIS: Ectopic endometrium located in various sites
throughout the pelvis or in the abdominal wall.

ENDOMETRITIS: Inflammation of the endometrium, the inner
mucous lining of the uterus.

ENTEROCOCCUS: Any species of steptococcus inhabiting the
intestine.

ERECTILE TISSUE: Vascular tissue that, when filled with
blood, becomes erect or rigid, as the clitoris, penis,
or nipples.

EROTICISM: Excessive libido; also, intense sexual desire.

ESTROGEN: Any natural or artificial substance that induces
estrogenic activity; hormone responsible for development
of secondary sexual characteristics.

ESTRUS: The recurrent period of sexual activity in mammals
other than primates, called "heat," characterized by
congestion of and secretions by the uterine mucosa,
proliferation of vaginal epithelium, swelling of vulva,
ovulation, and acceptance of the male by the female.

EUSTACHIAN TUBES: The auditory tube (from the middle ear to
the pharynx) lined with mucous membrane.

EXTRINSIC: From, or coming from, without.

FAG: Slang for male homosexual.

FALLOPIAN TUBE: Tube that transmits ova to the uterus.

FASCICULATE: Bundling of nerve or muscle fibers.

FEMALE TROUBLE: Slang term to denote infection or inflammation of the internal female organs.

FERTILIZED OVA: Ovum that has been impregnated with spermatozoa of the male; takes place in Fallopian tubes.

FIBRINOGEN: A protein present in blood plasm--essential for
blood clotting.

FIBRINOUS BRIDGE: Narrow band of tissue consisting of fibrin.

FIBRINOUS DEGENERATION: A form of deterioration of muscle
tissue in which its vitality is diminished.

FIBROIDS: Containing or resembling fibers; a colloquial term
for fibroma, especially fibroma of uterus.

FIBROMA: A fibrous, encapsulated, connective tissue tumor.

FIBROSIS: Abnormal formation of fibrous tissue.

FIBROUS: Composed of or containing fibers.

FIMBRIATED ENDS: Fringed.

FORMED ELEMENTS: Nonliquid contents of the blood, for example,
white blood cells, red cells, platelets, etc.

FRIGIDITY: In the female, absence of sexual desire. Inability to have an orgasm.

FUNDUS: The largest part, base, or body of a hollow organ.

The portion of an organ most remote from its opening; top of uterus.

FUNDUS OF UTERUS: The rounded portion of the body lying above the opening of the two uterine tubes.

GRAAFIAN FOLLICLES: Small sacs embedded in the cortex of the ovary that contain ova, or egg cells.

GRAVIDITY: Pregnancy.

GRAVITY: The force of the earth's gravitational attraction.

GYNECOID: Wide pelvis, as in white females, contrasted to the anthropoid pelvis, as in black females.

GYNEFOLD: Form of pessary for lifting fundus of uterus anteriorly from vagina.

HOMOPLANT: Having similar form and structure (Homoplastic); homoplant: to transfer within same individual.

HORMONE: A substance, originating in an organ, gland, or part, that is conveyed usually through the blood to another part of the body.

HOT FLASHES: Crisis of vasodilation in skin of head, neck and chest, accompanied by sensation of suffocation and sweating; occurs commonly during menopause.

HUMEROL: Formed elements of the blood.

HYDROSALPINX: Distention of Fallopian tube by clear fluid.

HYPERTENSION: A condition in which patient has a higher blood pressure than that judged to be normal.

HYSTERECTOMY: Removal of the uterus.

ILEUS: A form of intestinal obstruction, due to nonmechanical causes, for example, paralytic bowel obstruction.

INCUBATE: The interval between exposure to infection and the appearance of the first symptom; the development of an impregnated ovum.

INDIGENOUS BACTERIA: Bacteria native to its region.

INFECTION: State or condition in which the body or a part of it is invaded by a pathogenic agent (microorganism or virus) that, under favorable conditions, multiplies and produces effects that are injurious.

INFLAMMATION: Tissue reaction to injury, the succession of changes that occur in living tissue when it is injured.

INNERVATE: As the nerve supply of an organ.

INTERNAL GENITALIA: Female; two ovaries, Fallopian tubes, uterus, and vagina.

INTROITUS: An opening or entrance into a canal or cavity, as the vagina.

LIBIDO: The sexual drive, conscious or unconscious.

LOWER BRAIN: Below cerebrum, for example, pons, medulla, cerebellum, etc.

MALIGNANT: Virulent; growing worse; resisting treatment, said of cancerous growths.

MEDULLARY: Concerning marrow or medulla.

MENARCHE: Onset of menses.

MENDELIAN DOMINANT: Of Mendel's Laws: law of dominance;
     in a pair of genes, one dominant and the other reces-
     sive, the dominant trait in an offspring will occur more
     often than the recessive one.
"MENNIES": Slang for monthlies or menses, or menopausal
     symptoms.
MENSES: Monthly flow of bloody fluid from the uterine mucous
     membrane.
MENSTRUM: Menstrual fluid and debris from uterus.
MISSIONARY WAY: Most traditional position for sexual inter-
     course; female in supine position, male on top.
MONOGAMOUS: The practice or state of being married to only
     one person at a time.
MORALS: Principles or standards with respect to right and
     wrong in conduct.
MORBIDITY: State of being diseased.
MORTAL: Causing death; subject to death; human.
MORTALITY: State of being mortal.
MUTATION: Change; transformation.
NABOTHIAN GLANDS: Dilated mucous glands in the uterine
     cervix.
"NOSE OPENED": Slang term to denote sexual gratification or
     climax exhibited by a feeling of exhilaration, for
     example, air rushing through sinuses whose passageway
     is opened. The morning-after feeling.
OOPHORECTOMY: Excision of an ovary.
ORGANISM: Any living thing, plant or animal.
ORGAN: Part of body having a special function.
ORGASM: A state of paroxysmal emotional excitement, especial-
     ly that which occurs at the climax of sexual inter-
     course; in the male it is accompanied by the ejaculation
     of semen; in the female, by a feeling of euphoria affect-
     ing several organs.
ORGASTIC: Concerning or related to sexual organs.
ORIFICE: Pertaining to or forming an orifice or opening.
OSTEOPOROSIS: Increased porosity of bone; softening of bone.
OVARIAN PLEXUS OF VESSELS: See Panpiniform.
OVARY: Organ that produces germ cells, or ova, in the female.
OVULATION: The periodic ripening and rupture of the mature
     Graafian follicle and discharge of the ovum from the
     cortex of the ovary.
PANPINIFORM: Network of veins lying in mesovarium and
     draining the ovary.
PARALYTIC BOWEL OBSTRUCTION: Paralysis of intestinal wall
     with distention and symptoms of acute obstruction and
     prostration. Etiology: it may occur after any abdominal
     operation; same as paralytic ileus.
PARAMOUR: A lover or mistress in an illicit relationship.
PARENCHYMAL: The essential parts of an organ that are con-

cerned with its function in contradistinction to its
framework. P. disease: disease affecting the principal
tissue of an organ. P. testis: the functional portion
of the testis, including the seminiferous tubules within
the lobules.

PATHOGENESIS: Origination and development of a disease.

PATHOGENS: A microorganism or substance capable of producing
a disease.

PATHOLOGY: The study of the changes caused by disease in the
structure or function of the body.

PATHOPHYSIOLOGICAL: Study of changes caused by disease in
normal body functions.

PAVLOV: Russian physiologist; winner of Nobel prize in
medicine in 1904; he is remembered particularly for his
work on conditioned response.

PAVLOV'S EXPERIMENTS: Classical conditioning was discovered
by Pavlov; conditioning applies to involuntary behavior,
particularly reflexes involuntary responses that are
elicited by stimuli.

PELVIC INFLAMMATION: Inflammation pertaining to the pelvis.

PESSARY: Device inserted into the vagina to function as a
supportive structure for the uterus or as a contraceptive
device.

PHALLUS: The penis.

PHILADELPHIA LAWYER: A shrewd or tricky lawyer.

PHILANDERING: To engage lightly in love affairs.

PHILOSOPHIZE: To think or reason like a philosopher; to
moralize, express truisms, etc.

PHYSIOGNOMY: Facial features and expressions; functioning
anatomy.

PHYSIOLOGICALLY: Concerning body function.

PING-PONGING: Passing of an infection (such as Trichomoniasis)
back and forth between partners before infection has
cleared up.

POLYGAMOUS: The practice of having two or more wives or
husbands at the same time.

POSTPARTUM: After childbirth.

POTENTIAL JOINTS: Latent joints; existing in possibility.

PREFRONTAL: The middle portion of the ethmoid bone; in anterior part of the frontal lobe of the brain.

PRESSURE HEAD: Kind of pressure exerted by a column of liquid.

PROCREATOR: One who brings forth young; one who begets.

PROGRAMMED THINKING: The use of existing systems of thought
without deviation.

PROMISCUOUS: Characterized by a lack of discrimination,
especially in sexual liaisons.

PROMISCUITY: Noun; promiscuous.

PROSTATE: Gland that secretes a substance that precedes the
spermatozoa and secretions of the seminal vesicles during

sexual intercourse.

PSYCHOLOGICAL: Pertains to study of the mind, in all of its relationships, normal or abnormal.

PUBOCOCCYGEUS MUSCLE: Levator Ani and Coccygeus Muscle, which together form floor of pelvic cavity; supports pelvic organs.

PULMONARY EMBOLI: Obstruction of the pulmonary (lung) artery or one of its branches by blood clot; usually from legs or pelvis.

PYOSALPINX: Pus in the fallopian tube.

QUADRUPED: Four-footed animal; assuming a position with hands and feet on floor.

RECIPIENT (TRANSPLANT): One who receives anything, especially those who receive blood, tissues, or organs provided by a donor.

RECTUM: Lower part of large intestine between sigmoid flexure and the anal canal.

RETROFLEXION: A bending or flexing backward.

ROUND LIGAMENTS: Two round cordlike structures passing from front of the body of the uterus in the anterior wall of broad ligament, below the Fallopian tubes, outward through the inguinal canals to soft tissues of the labia majora.

SACROILIAC JOINTS: The articulation between the hipbone and sacrum.

SACRUM: The triangular bone situated behind and inferior from the two ilia between the 5th lumbar vertebrae and coccyx.

"SAPPHIRISH": Slang for evil black female; sapphism: seventh century, female homosexuality. Sappho was the reputed instigator of lesbianism.

SEPTICEMIA: Morbid condition from absorption of septic products into blood and tissue or of pathogenic bacteria that rapidly multiply. Syn.: blood poisoning.

SEQUELLA: A condition following and resulting from a disease.

SICKLE CELL: Abnormal red blood corpuscle of crescent shape.

SPAY: Surgical removal of ovaries, usually said of animals.

STAGNATION: Cessation of motion; in pathology, a stoppage of motion of any fluid in the body, as blood.

STAPHYLOCOCCUS: A genus of micrococci belonging to the family of Micrococcacaea. They are gram positive. Some species are pathogenic. Some cause a type of food poisoning.

STENOSIS: Constriciton or narrowing of a passage or orifice.

STERILITY: Inability to produce offspring.

SUBCEREBRATE: Pertaining to region beneath largest part of brain (cerebrum).

SUBCORTICAL: Pertaining to the region beneath the cerebral cortex.

TAMPON: A roll or pack made of various absorbent substances used to arrest hemorrhage or absorb secretions from a wound or body cavity.

TAMPONADE: To use or make use of a tampon.

"TART": Slang for prostitute.

TESTOSTERONE: Male hormone that stimulates and promotes the growth of secondary sexual characteristics and is essential for normal sexual behavior and the occurrence of erections.

TRANSPLANTATION: The taking of a portion of living tissue from its normal position in the body or from the body of another person and uniting it with like tissue in another place to lessen defect or remedy deformity or injury.

TUBE: A cylinder-shaped hollow organ.

TURBINATES: Cone-shaped bone, that is, nasal conchae, three scroll-shaped bones that project medially from the lateral wall of the nasal cavity.

URETERS: Two tubes that carry urine from the kidneys to the bladder.

URETHRAL STENOSIS: Constriction of urethra (a canal for the discharge of urine extending from the bladder to the outside).

UTERUS: An organ of the female for containing and nourishing the embryo and fetus from the time the fertilized egg is implanted to the time of birth of fetus.

VENEREAL DISEASE: Disease acquired ordinarily as a result of sexual intercourse with an individual who is afflicted. The diseases are gonorrhea, syphillis, and chancroid, trichomonas vaginalis vaginitis.

VIRULENT BACTERIA: Very poisonous; infectious bacteria.

VIS-A-VIS: In relation to.

VISCOSITY: State of being sticky or gummy.

VULVA: That portion of the female genitalia lying beneath the mons veneris consisting of labia majora, labia minora, clitoris, vestibule of the vagina, and bulbs of the vestibule.

WESTERN CIVILIZATION: Total culture of Western hemispheres (that half of the earth including North and South America including Europe).